box

in the

classic and traditional box designs
15 step-by-step woodworking projects

A L A N   A N D   G I L L   B R I D G E W A T E R

NEW
HOLLAND

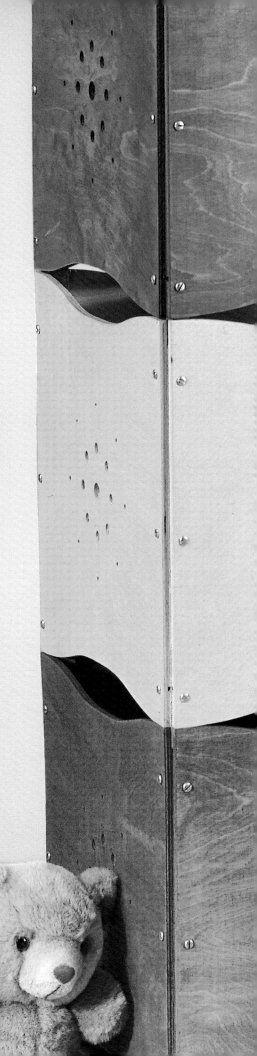

First published in 2001 by New Holland Publishers (UK) Ltd
London • Cape Town • Sydney • Auckland

Garfield House, 86 Edgware Road, London W2 2EA, United Kingdom

80 McKenzie Street, Cape Town, 8001, South Africa

Level 1, Unit 4, 14 Aquatic Drive, Frenchs Forest, NSW 2086, Australia

218 Lake Road, Northcote, Auckland, New Zealand

10 9 8 7 6 5 4 3 2 1

ISBN 1 85974 443 5 (hb)
ISBN 1 85974 444 3 (pb)

Editorial direction: Rosemary Wilkinson
Project editor: Kate Latham
Production: Caroline Hansell

Designed and created for New Holland by AG&G BOOKS
Design: Glyn Bridgewater
Illustrators: Alan and Gill Bridgewater
Box design: Glyn Bridgewater
Photography: Ian Parsons
Editor: Fiona Corbridge
Woodwork: Glyn and Alan Bridgewater
Wood species: The Art Veneers Co. Ltd

Reproduction by Modern Age Repro House Ltd, Hong Kong
Printed and bound in Malaysia by Times Offset (M) sdn Bhd

CONVERSION CHART

To convert the metric measurements given in this book to imperial measurements, simply multiply the figure given in the text by the relevant number shown in the table below. Bear in mind that conversions will not necessarily work out exactly, and you will need to round the figure up or down slightly. (Do not use a combination of metric and imperial measurements – for accuracy, keep to one system.)

To convert	Multiply by
millimetres to inches	0.0394
metres to feet	3.28
metres to yards	1.093
sq millimetres to sq inches	0.00155
sq metres to sq feet	10.76
sq metres to sq yards	1.195
cu metres to cu feet	35.31
cu metres to cu yards	1.308
grams to pounds	0.0022
kilograms to pounds	2.2046
litres to gallons	0.22

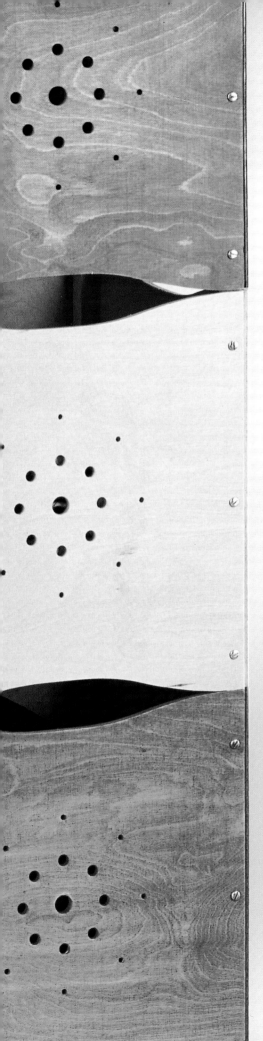

CONTENTS

INTRODUCTION

Boxes are uniquely personal pieces of furniture, which are used for keeping, storing and concealing things. At some time or other, just about everything we value is kept in a box. They are also objects of intrigue: when most people see a box, they have an almost overwhelming desire to lift the lid to see what's inside.

There is an old adage that says that a box symbolizes all the qualities of home and family. One image this brings to mind is that of families moving from the Old World to the American West in carts and wagons, with all their prized possessions in a single, precious family chest. Perhaps a box has an uncomplicated directness and truth about it, which equates with family values.

From the woodworker's point of view, the exciting aspect of making a box is the knowledge that it is almost certainly going to be around for a long time. A box isn't at the mercy of fashion in the same way as, for example, a kitchen cupboard – it just sits quietly in a corner and gets used. You only have to look in antique shops and fleamarkets to see that boxes survive through the generations.

Because they anticipate that the boxes will be passed down through the generations, woodworkers have traditionally put a lot of effort into making and decorating them. A good box usually has lots of carefully cut joints and painstaking details, with the inside and underside being given as much consideration as the sides on view.

We have designed the projects so that they can be made by woodworkers of all levels, from inexperienced beginners with only a basic tool kit, to those who are more accomplished. The projects are graded so that beginners will be able to build up their knowledge and confidence gradually.

We show, with hands-on detail, how to make fifteen different classic and traditional forms. Projects range from a simple folk art wall box that can be made with not much more than a hammer and nails, to a beautiful Arts and Crafts oak blanket box complete with complex dovetail joints and laminated handles. And of course if you want to make a straightforward, basic functional plywood and batten box, we tell you how.

Each project opens with an introduction that puts the piece in context, describing the inspiration behind it and its main features. This is followed by a section that analyses the design considerations, discussing how it is made, the main tools and techniques. Then we go straight into the making stages, where clear, concise text tells you exactly what to do. There are extensive tool and cutting lists, and traditional working drawings, together with design variations, a troubleshooting section to sort out problems, and colour photographs to guide you through the construction process. At all stages we tell you just about all that there is to know about the project. If you are at all uncertain about using a particular tool or constructing a joint, or you want to use a different wood, then the "Tools, Materials and Techniques" section will help.

So, there's no longer any excuse for stuffing tatty plastic bin liners full of belongings under the bed, or filling up disintegrating cardboard boxes with clothes. Now you can build boxes to suit your every need. And of course, the boxes are not just functional – they are objects to be admired.

Alan & Gill

HEALTH AND SAFETY

Woodworking procedures are potentially dangerous. Before starting work check through the following list:

- Make sure you are not going to get dragged into machines. Tie back hair, roll up sleeves and remove jewellery.
- Follow the manufacturer's instructions when making adjustments to machines.
- Make sure guards are in place (some photographs in this book show guards removed for clarity).

- Never use machines if you are overtired.
- Make sure all electrics conform to recommended standards.
- Wear a dust-mask and goggles.
- When using MDF, wear a dust-mask and use a dust extractor.
- When using chisels, always cut away from your body.
- Keep a first-aid kit and telephone within easy reach.

About this book

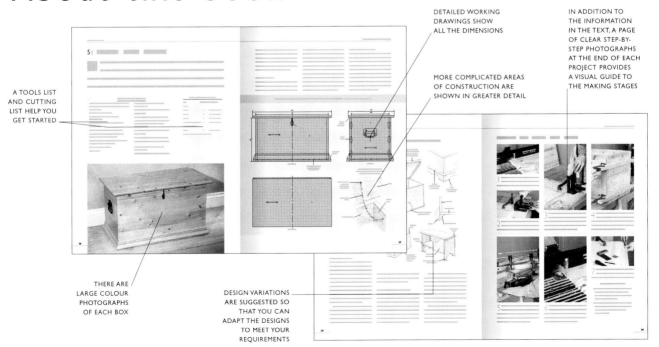

A TOOLS LIST AND CUTTING LIST HELP YOU GET STARTED

THERE ARE LARGE COLOUR PHOTOGRAPHS OF EACH BOX

DESIGN VARIATIONS ARE SUGGESTED SO THAT YOU CAN ADAPT THE DESIGNS TO MEET YOUR REQUIREMENTS

DETAILED WORKING DRAWINGS SHOW ALL THE DIMENSIONS

MORE COMPLICATED AREAS OF CONSTRUCTION ARE SHOWN IN GREATER DETAIL

IN ADDITION TO THE INFORMATION IN THE TEXT, A PAGE OF CLEAR STEP-BY-STEP PHOTOGRAPHS AT THE END OF EACH PROJECT PROVIDES A VISUAL GUIDE TO THE MAKING STAGES

PART ONE

Tools, materials and techniques

Woodworking is a wonderfully exciting and therapeutic activity – you can enjoy the smell and feel of the wood, and the sense of achievement when you use an item that you have made yourself. The size of your workshop is not really important – you might be working in the garage or a shed in the garden. However, it is necessary to understand the options for tools, techniques and materials. You have to appreciate why, in the context of the task in hand, a particular tool, wood type or technique is better than another.

SMALL MACHINES, POWER TOOLS AND HAND TOOLS

Wood is commonly sold just sawn or planed, but many suppliers are willing to cut it to the customer's specifications. However, if you like the idea of preparing your own wood, you will need a planer-thicknesser and a table saw. To make the boxes in this book, we recommend the machines and tools illustrated below. If you do not have a table saw and a planer-thicknesser, see page 12 for alternative ways of preparing wood.

MACHINE PLANING

Machine planing involves surfacing the timber to square up the face side and face edge, and thicknessing it to plane the remaining surfaces true to the face side and face edge.

A planer-thicknesser is used for surface planing and for thicknessing.

TABLE SAW

A table saw is used for cutting planed wood and plywood to size quickly and accurately. A hand-held circular saw and radial arm saw together perform similar tasks.

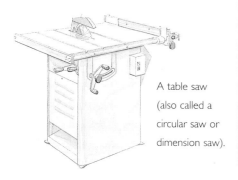

A table saw (also called a circular saw or dimension saw).

SAWS FOR CUTTING CURVES

There are three basic machine-sawing options for cutting curves in wood: a bandsaw for cutting broad, clean curves in thick wood, a scroll saw for cutting tight, intricate curves in thin wood and a hand-held power jigsaw for cutting coarse curves in sheet board and thin wood.

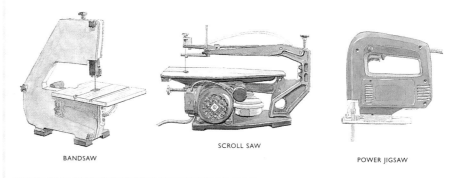

BANDSAW

SCROLL SAW

POWER JIGSAW

MEASURING AND MARKING

You will need a tape measure and ruler for setting out measurements, a straight-edge for drawing straight lines, a square for drawing right angles, a bevel gauge for marking angles, a single-pin marking gauge for setting out joints, a marking knife (or craft knife) for scoring lines and a pencil.

SQUARE

COMBINED MARKING KNIFE (LEFT END) AND SCRATCH AWL (RIGHT END)

SINGLE-PIN MARKING GAUGE

ROUTER

Using a router is a fast way of cutting grooves, housings, rebates and edge profiles. A huge range of cutters is available – the most common are straight cutters. Purchase individual cutters to suit the task in hand.

A router mounted in a router table is the easiest and safest option when you are working with small pieces of wood (300 mm long or less).

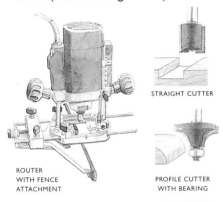

ROUTER
WITH FENCE
ATTACHMENT

STRAIGHT CUTTER

PROFILE CUTTER
WITH BEARING

BISCUIT JOINTER

A biscuit jointer cuts small grooves to make dowel-like joints. Instead of dowels fitting into drilled holes, flat plates of wood called biscuits are glued into corresponding slots.

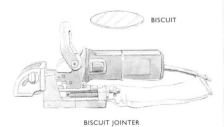

BISCUIT

BISCUIT JOINTER

CHISELS

Chisels are used in joint-making. It is best to start out with four bevel-edged chisels in a range of sizes: 6.6 mm, 9.5 mm, 16 mm and 25 mm.

The bevel-edged chisel is designed for general paring and joint-making.

HAND SAWS

Backsaws (available in different sizes) are used in joint-making. The coping saw too is used in jointing and also for cutting curves. A mitre saw (a saw set within a jig) cuts a variety of set angles, the most useful being 45°.

BACKSAW

MITRE SAW

CLAMPS

Sash clamps and G-clamps (and their derivatives) are used to hold wood secure as you work, and to clamp joints together during gluing. A hold-fast (inserted through a hole in the workbench) is used to grip wood so it does not move while you work on it.

SASH CLAMP

G-CLAMP   HOLDFAST

HAND PLANES

In this book we use just three planes: a smoothing plane for working edges and faces to a smooth finish, a block plane for tidying up end grain and a spokeshave for working curves and round sections.

SMOOTHING
PLANE

DRILLING

Woodworkers need to bore holes. Ideally, you need a bench drill press, a hand-held electric drill and a good selection of twist bits and forstner bits (for large-diameter holes).

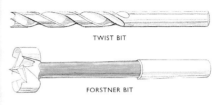

TWIST BIT

FORSTNER BIT

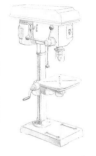

A bench drill press is the ideal machine for boring accurate holes.

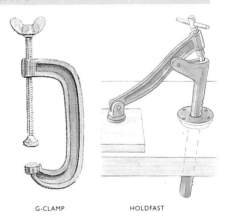

BLOCK PLANE

The spokeshave is used for planing convex and concave curves (depending on the sole).

MATERIALS AND WOOD TYPES

A major part of the joy of working with wood is the fact that every piece of wood you are crafting is unique. However, in order to avoid potential problems, you need to be aware of the characteristics of various materials before you buy – the good, the bad and the ugly!

TIMBER

If you own a circular saw and a planer-thicknesser, you can buy rough-sawn boards from a timber merchant and cut and plane all the sections described in a cutting list. Otherwise, find a supplier who will prepare the wood for you and give him a cutting list. A range of ready-prepared wood can be bought from DIY merchants, but to use this you may have to alter a design to suit the sections available.

Extra-wide boards (such as for the side of a chest) are normally achieved by gluing together a number of narrower boards (see page 15).

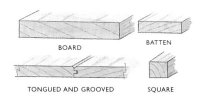

BOARD   BATTEN

TONGUED AND GROOVED   SQUARE

Examples of ready-prepared sections.

FAULTS IN TIMBER

Timber is always less than perfect. Part of the skill of woodworking is being able to identify the faults that cannot be accommodated within the structure of a project, and to reject unsuitable wood before you pay for it. Plywood is usually free from faults, but check there are no patched knots and that the board is not warped.

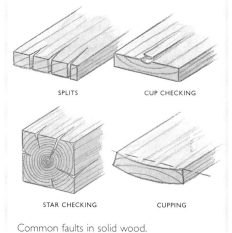

SPLITS   CUP CHECKING

STAR CHECKING   CUPPING

Common faults in solid wood.

PLYWOOD AND VENEER

Many types of plywood are available, for example coarse-centred Malaysian ply, various thick-cut plies, and an assortment of other types in between. For making boxes, we recommend top-quality birch veneer-core or multi-ply plywood. This is expensive, but the advantage of it is that the edges are capable of being taken to a perfectly smooth finish.

If we need to laminate a small component part, such as the "bridge" handles used on the Arts and Crafts Blanket Box (page 60), we use constructional veneer (about 1.6 mm thick) bonded with PVA glue. A thinner veneer (0.6 mm thick) can be glued to plywood to give the appearance of solid wood. Different varieties of veneer can be assembled in decorative patterns like the one on the Marquetry Jewellery Box (page 48).

ALLOWING FOR MOVEMENT IN WOOD

Wood shrinks and expands according to atmospheric conditions (movement is greater across the width than along the length). Part of the designing and building procedure involves minimizing and/or disguising the effects of movement. Slotted screw fixings, frame and loose-panel construction, sliding joints and cover-up grooves are all methods of coping with it.

The stopped housing ensures that movement within the joint is hidden.

A tongue-and-groove construction also helps to disguise movement.

TYPES OF WOOD

There are many thousands of species of tree, the wood of which varies greatly in size, colour and working characteristics. The secret of good woodwork is being able to choose a piece of wood that you know for sure is going to suit the intended purpose. It is helpful to study the work of woodworkers of previous generations, to see how the wood has been used and in what context. We have taken our lead from European and American woodworkers, in that we have chosen to use a small range of non-endangered native species that have traditionally been used for building boxes and chests. Always choose your wood with care. If the pieces on offer look in any way uncharacteristic – poor colour or wild grain – look for another source.

American maple: A creamy-coloured, close-grained, smooth-textured, difficult-to-work hardwood. Cuts cleanly and produces a fair finish. Readily available in good, knot-free widths and lengths.

European pine: A creamy to pinkish yellow-brown, straight-grained, coarse-textured, knotty softwood. A good choice for experimental forms, and for bold, naïve designs. Readily available at low cost.

American cherry: A straight-grained, fine-textured, creamy pinkish-brown hardwood. It works to a high-shine finish – which is perfect for hand tool work – but it does tend to blunt tools quickly.

English cherry: A cream to pinky-brown, strong-textured hardwood. Works to a dynamic high-shine finish. Coarser and available in smaller widths and lengths than its American cousin.

European birch: A pale cream to yellow-brown, straight-grained, strong and stable, easy-to-work hardwood. Readily available in generous widths and lengths. Easy to stain and colour-wash. A good choice of material for beginners who lack confidence.

Cedar: Known as "true" cedar, Mount Lebanon cedar also has many other names. A brown, straight-grained softwood. Traditionally, cedar is used for top-quality interior joinery and furniture. Many cedars give off a pleasant aroma.

English larch: A pinkish, browny-white, straight-grained, resinous, even-textured softwood. Available in good widths and lengths. The wood is difficult to work, but compensates by being very flexible and strong along its length.

English beech: A straight-grained, even-textured, brownish-white hardwood. Available in many widths and lengths. Excellent for planing and jointing, and for making shelves. It works to a hard, smooth, waxy finish.

Douglas fir: A reddish-brown, straight, coarse-grained softwood, available in good widths and lengths. Sticky and prone to splitting, but has an exciting grain pattern, and is strong in long lengths.

American red oak: A pinky-brown, biscuit-coloured, coarse, straight-grained hardwood. Available in good, knot-free widths and lengths. Good for shelves. Relatively easy to work, and finishes well.

JOINTS AND FIXING

Some woodworkers consider jointing to be no more than a means to an end – a procedure that is concerned with working out how best to join a number of pieces of wood. But others believe that the total involvement of hand, eye and mind in making the joints is an end in itself.

TYPES OF JOINT *All the joints below (except the nailed and screwed joints) are glued and clamped once made*

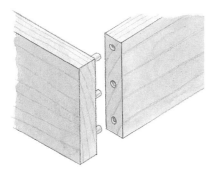

Dowel joint
The dowel joint is a butt joint fixed with pegs that are pushed into aligned holes drilled into the mating parts. The dowel is a swift solution – it is more attractive than a screw, but not as aesthetically pleasing as a dovetail.

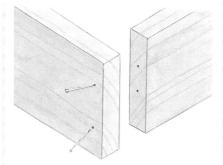

Butt nailed joint
A butt nailed joint is no more than a swift hammer and nails job. The angled nails, used in conjunction with glue, create a strong joint that does not easily come apart. This joint is good for boxes in a folk art style.

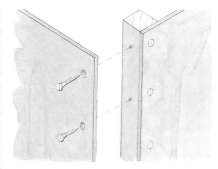

Screwed batten joint
This joint has long been favoured by folk art woodworkers – especially by box builders – for the simple reason that it is quick and easy. The battens need to be planed with care so the joints will fit together closely.

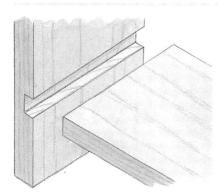

Through housing joint
The through housing joint is favoured by box builders for drawers and partitions, not only because the easy-to-make design allows for movement, but also because it is strong, and it can be cut with a machine.

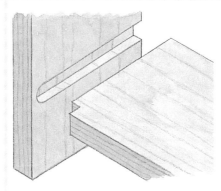

Stopped housing joint
The stopped housing joint is the same as a housing joint, but the groove stops short of the edge of the board. The structure of the joint results in the groove being hidden from view.

Through dovetail joint
The through dovetail is a traditional joint for joining box sides, and has a visually exciting design. It results in an extremely strong structure that cannot easily be pulled apart, and is perfect for box-making.

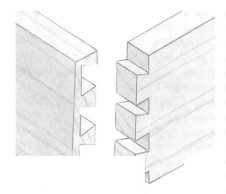

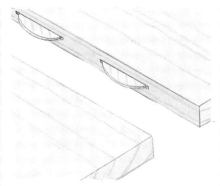

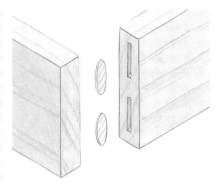

t

used in box-
as drawer
re a dovetail
ength, but the
to be hidden
vith the pins
tails.

Biscuit edge-to-edge joint

The biscuit edge-to-edge joint works
in much the same way as the dowel
edge joint. However, the biscuit
jointing procedure gives the woodworker some leeway in putting the
joint together – unlike the dowel edge
joint, where precision is vital.

Biscuit butt joint

The biscuit butt joint is similar to a
dowel butt joint. Biscuits are pushed
into aligned holes in the mating parts.
However, the biscuit joint is much
easier to make, and the action of the
biscuits swelling in the grooves results
in a much stronger joint.

NTS

ust the right
pe of glue, is
gth of most
idea to have
luing, so you
and generally
ork.

USING SCREWS

For making boxes from a mixture of
solid wood and plywood (where
plywood sides are screwed to corner
battens) or for functional boxes that
need to be built in a hurry, screws are
a great idea. Whatever the type of
screw, the secret of success is to use a
screw of the correct length, and to
drill a pilot hole prior to driving the
screw home. To prevent damage to
the screw, always use a screwdriver
that fits the head of the screw.

HINGES

Box builders tend to use either good-
quality butt hinges, with the flaps
screwed to the top edge of the box
and the underside of the face or edge
of the lid, or decorative strap hinges
that have both flaps in full view.

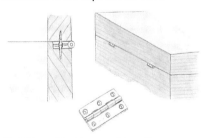

Butt hinges fitted to a small box. You can
recess the whole thickness of the hinge into
the base so that the lid is not weakened.

Spread the glue evenly on both mating
surfaces of the joint.

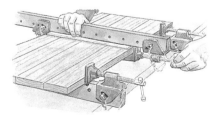

Clamp up, placing a piece of paper between
the clamp and the workpiece. Tighten until a
bead of glue oozes out of the joint.

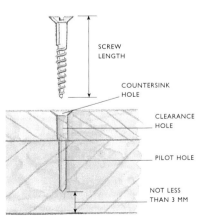

SCREW
LENGTH

COUNTERSINK
HOLE

CLEARANCE
HOLE

PILOT HOLE

NOT LESS
THAN 3 MM

The length of a screw should be three times
the thickness of the piece being fixed.

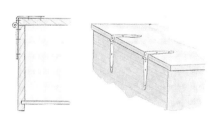

Strap hinges are ideal for hinging the lid of a
chest, as they are strong and decorative. You
may need to bend one side of the hinge.

FINISHING MATERIALS AND TECHNIQUES

The finishing process is lots of fun and very exciting. One moment you have a brand-new, plain pine wall box, and a few hours later – after several coats of acrylic paint, with lots of rubbing down followed by a burnishing with beeswax polish – you have an item that looks a hundred years old.

PLANING END GRAIN

Once you have put a box together, it is usually necessary to work the end grain to a good finish. Using a plane in conjunction with a piece of waste allows the plane to run through without splitting the grain.

Clamp the waste wood to the side of the workpiece – so that it receives the brunt as the plane runs through.

SANDING

Sanding, or rubbing down, is the technique of using graded abrasive paper to cut back the fibres of the wood to a smooth finish. Abrasive paper is sold according to grit size, with the smallest grit producing the finest cut.

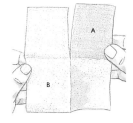

Use sandpaper wrapped around a block of wood to sand flat surfaces to a fine finish. Work with the grain.

SANDPAPER FITS OVER FOAM PAD

An orbital power sander leaves a finish that requires the minimum of hand sanding.

Use sandpaper on its own for delicate work. Fold and tear as shown and then refold so that "A" overlaps "B".

SCRAPING

Scraper planes and cabinet scrapers are used to remove torn grain, machine plane ripples and other damaged areas. A sharp scraper leaves a beautifully burnished finish.

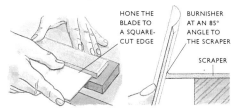

HONE THE BLADE TO A SQUARE-CUT EDGE

BURNISHER AT AN 85° ANGLE TO THE SCRAPER

SCRAPER

To sharpen a cabinet scraper, use a medium sharpening stone to hone the blade. Hold the scraper flat on the bench and run a burnisher at an angle to create a burr.

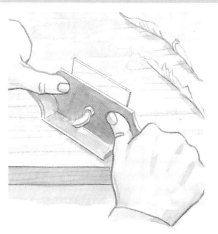

To use the scraper plane, it is held with two hands and run at a shearing angle to the direction of the grain.

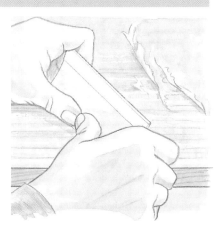

Cabinet scrapers are flexible and are invaluable when you need to smooth out small areas of damaged grain.

DANISH OIL AND BEESWAX

Oil and beeswax give a wonderfully fast and easy finish. You do not have to worry about runs, dribbles and brush-marks, there are no concerns about toxic vapours, and the finish will not crack or flake. We favour using a traditional mixture of beeswax (make sure that it is pure) and turpentine. Always read the label and avoid products that include "other waxes".

2 Wipe the surface with a cloth soaked in Danish oil and let it dry.

1 Vacuum up the dust, brush off the surface and wipe over with a clean cotton cloth. Carry out a final check for small blobs of glue (sand off if found).

3 Rub a small amount of beeswax into the surface. Finally, use a lint-free cotton cloth to burnish the wood to a deep, mellow shine.

VARNISH

A varnished surface is hardwearing and waterproof, so is a good choice for tabletops, where cups of liquid may get knocked over. It comes in a matt, sheen or high-gloss finish. We favour diluting the varnish with white spirit, and laying it on in several thin coats.

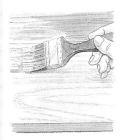

1 Thin a small quantity of the varnish with white spirit, and brush it on in the direction of the grain.

2 Rub down with fine sandpaper, wipe the dust away and brush on a final undiluted coat of varnish.

ALTERNATIVE FINISHING EFFECTS

Wire brushing

Using a wire brush fitted to a drill is a fast and dynamic way of creating a surface that looks as if it has been weathered – bleached by the sun and rain, and scoured by wind-driven sand.

1 Use an electric drill fitted with a rotary steel brush to remove areas of soft grain.

2 Use a hand brush to exaggerate the texture on selected corners and edges.

Colour-washing

A thin wash of colour, usually made up from acrylic paint or powder pigments mixed with water, is brushed on in the direction of the grain, to create a naïve, folk art effect.

1 Brush the paint so the colour is thicker in the corners and centre of the piece.

2 Sand the surface to cut through the paint in some places. Wax to a shine finish.

Ageing

Ageing is the procedure of breaking down the finish in order to create a surface that looks as if it is timeworn – the result of many years of wear and tear, sunlight and polishing.

1 Colour-wash, sand and wax the surface. Sand through the finish on sharp edges.

2 Cut through areas of wax with various items and re-burnish with tinted wax.

PART TWO

Projects

Boxes are, to a great extent, immune from the vagaries of fashion. They tend to become much-loved heirlooms and, as such, invite personalization, such as painted initials and dates or carved features.

The best way to tackle the projects is to study the drawings and then to consider the design and the procedures in the light of your skills, tool kit and requirements. The design variations show you how the projects can be transformed into something a little different. Or you may have your own ideas for adapting the designs, such as using more ornate hinges, or applying a bolder finish. There is plenty of scope for creative input!

1: SHAKER WALL BOX

T his beautifully simple cutlery box draws its inspiration from the furniture made by the Shakers of the South Union Community in Kentucky, in the last quarter of the nineteenth century. The design is low-key yet sophisticated, and it looks quite at home in a modern kitchen.

TOOLS AND MATERIALS

- workbench, fitted with a vice and holdfast
- square, tape measure, ruler, pencil, tracing paper
- backsaw
- scroll saw
- electric drill, 6 mm twist bit
- pin hammer
- long-nose pliers
- power sander and graded sandpaper
- pins: 16 x 16 mm long
- white candle
- acrylic paint in colour to suit, paintbrush
- PVA glue
- Danish oil and beeswax polish
- birch plywood (see cutting list)

CUTTING LIST

part	quantity	L x W x T
birch plywood back (A)	1	360 x 120 x 6
birch plywood front (B)	1	180 x 120 x 6
birch plywood sides (C)	2	180 x 108 x 6
birch plywood base (D)	1	108 x 108 x 6

(finished sizes, given in millimetres)

WORKING DRAWINGS AND DETAIL OF THE SHAKER WALL BOX
measurements are given in millimetres

120

20 mm grid

180

A

360

180

B

C

FRONT VIEW

SIDE VIEW

6 108 6

6

108

D

6

PLAN VIEW

EXPLODED VIEW SHOWING
THE GENERAL CONSTRUCTION

HOLE FOR
MOUNTING
ON WALL

BACK
BOARD

POSITION OF PINS

SIDE

FRONT

BASE

The box is wonderfully easy to make — there are only five boards of plywood, which are butted, glued, and fixed with brass pins. We designed the box to hold wooden cooking utensils and to complement our modern stainless-steel kitchen. If you are looking for a wall box that fits into a contemporary setting, yet harks back to older traditions, this Shaker design is perfect. We have chosen to give the box a simple, rounded back board and paint it a delicate blue-green colour, but you could modify the shape of the back to make it more decorative, or paint the box in a colour to suit your own colour scheme. Instead of one plain hole for mounting the box, you could make this necessity more of a feature by fretting a pattern or motif into the whole of the back board.

Design notes

This attractive box is made from five sheets of plywood — the back board, the front, two sides and the base. The back board is fretted to shape the delicate rounded profile and the hanging hole, and the whole thing is held together with glue and brass pins, with the side boards being captured between the front and the back board.

The subtle, sheen finish is achieved by brushing on a thin coat of acrylic paint and letting it dry, rubbing through to reveal the grain, laying on a coat of Danish oil and then burnishing with beeswax. It is most important, when you come to the final rubbing down, that you wait until the paint is completely dry, so that the nibs of grain rise as dry hairs, and can be sanded off. If you prefer to practise the finishing techniques before working on the box, take one of the pieces of offcut plywood and work through the procedures as described.

Setting out the design

Check the plywood to make sure that there are no cavities and delaminations. Use the scroll saw to square the wood to length and width. Draw the back on tracing paper, making sure that the curve is symmetrical. Use a hard pencil to press-transfer the profile through to the wood. Mark the position of the hanging hole (step 1).

Drilling and fretting

Drill a pilot hole for the hanging hole with the 6 mm twist bit (step 2).

To shape the back board, fit the scroll saw with a new blade and rub the saw table with a white candle in order to reduce the wood-to-metal friction to a minimum. Switch on the power and gently feed the workpiece forward, presenting the jiggling blade with the line of cut. Always cut slightly to the waste side of the drawn line. Unhitch the saw blade, pass it through the pilot hole, refit and re-tension the blade, and cut out the hanging hole. At the end of the cut, be careful that the piece of waste does not jump up and get snagged between the saw arm and the workpiece. If the blade burns the wood, fit a new one (step 3).

Putting together

Join the back board to the two sides by gluing the mating surfaces to each other. Holding the pins with the long-nose pliers, use the pin hammer to fix the boards together with three pins along each edge. Make sure that the pins are spaced equally (step 4).

Glue the edges of the base board and set it in place between the back and side boards. Hammer pins through the sides and back and into the base to hold it firm (step 5).

Finally, put the box on its back, smear glue on the front edges of the side boards and base, position the front board and fix it with pins, hammering down into the edges of the sides and base. Leave the heads of the pins slightly proud, for decorative effect. Use a damp cloth to wipe away all traces of glue. Sand all the corners and edges with the power sander and sandpaper. When you sand the curved back and pierced hole, roll the sander over the sawn edges to achieve a rounded profile (step 6).

Finishing

Mix the acrylic paint with water to make a thin wash and give all inner and outer surfaces a couple of coats. When the paint is dry, use a sheet of fine-grade sandpaper to rub down all the nibs of grain to a smooth finish. Rub through the paint on selected edges and surfaces in order to create a worn finish. Finally, brush on a thin coat of Danish oil. Burnish to a sheen with beeswax polish.

DESIGN VARIATIONS

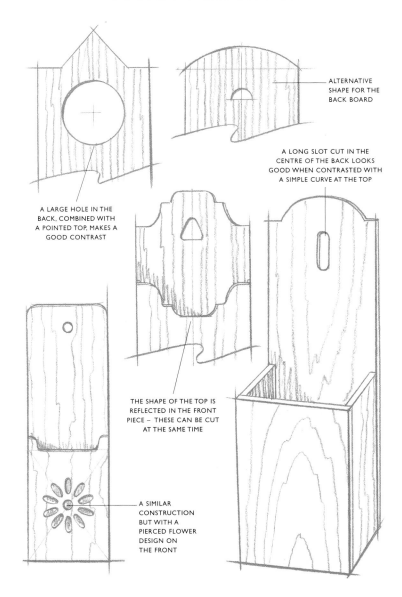

ALTERNATIVE SHAPE FOR THE BACK BOARD

A LONG SLOT CUT IN THE CENTRE OF THE BACK LOOKS GOOD WHEN CONTRASTED WITH A SIMPLE CURVE AT THE TOP

A LARGE HOLE IN THE BACK, COMBINED WITH A POINTED TOP, MAKES A GOOD CONTRAST

THE SHAPE OF THE TOP IS REFLECTED IN THE FRONT PIECE – THESE CAN BE CUT AT THE SAME TIME

A SIMILAR CONSTRUCTION BUT WITH A PIERCED FLOWER DESIGN ON THE FRONT

MAKING THE SHAKER WALL BOX

1 Setting out the back board
Draw the shape of the back on tracing paper. Flip the tracing over, align it with a centre line drawn on the back board, and press-transfer the tracing through.

2 Drilling holes
Fit the 6 mm twist bit in the electric drill. Set the workpiece on a piece of wood to prevent damage when the bit exits, and run the hole through.

3 Fretting out the back board
Wax the scroll saw table to reduce friction, and make sure that the blade is well tensioned. Cut slightly to the waste side of the drawn line.

6 Pinning the front board
Smear glue on the edges of the side boards, position and pin the front board.

TROUBLESHOOTING

- Always make sure that you have a stock of spare blades for the scroll saw. This avoids a frustrating delay if the blade snaps and you have to go and buy a new one.

- If you are not very good at hammering in pins, drill pilot holes prior to nailing.

4 Pinning the sides
Smear glue on the edges of the side boards, and bridge them with the back board. Nail the back board: pins must run right into the thickness of the wood.

5 Pinning the base board
Glue the edges of the base board and place it between the back and sides. Drive pins through side and back boards, and into the edge of the base board.

2: NESTING STORAGE BOXES

In our house, we are often in desperate need of boxes to store our collectibles. Then we have a clear-out, leaving us with empty boxes that take up valuable space. The good thing about these nesting storage boxes is that when they are empty, they can be stacked inside each other, like Russian dolls.

TOOLS AND MATERIALS

- workbench, fitted with a vice and holdfast
- square, tape measure, ruler, pencil
- backsaw
- screwdrivers: cross-point and flat
- router, router table, 6 mm groove cutter
- jigsaw and mitre saw
- bench drill press and forstner drill bits, 15 mm and 38 mm
- electric drill, 5 mm twist bit, rotary wire brush
- power sander and graded sandpaper
- screws: 68 x 30 mm cross-headed countersunk screws
- emulsion paint in green-grey, paintbrush
- Danish oil or matt varnish and beeswax polish
- rope, 380 mm long and 13 mm thick (makes 2 handles)
- PVA glue
- pine and birch plywood (see cutting list)

CUTTING LIST

part	quantity	L x W x T
large lid (A)	1	500 x 400 x 18
medium lid (B)	1	416 x 316 x 18
small lid (C)	1	332 x 232 x 18
large front/back (D)	2	500 x 282 x 18
medium front/back (E)	2	416 x 238 x 18
small front/back (F)	2	332 x 194 x 18
large sides (G)	2	364 x 282 x 18
medium sides (H)	2	280 x 238 x 18
small sides (I)	2	196 x 194 x 18
large side battens (J)	4	264 x 18 x 18
medium side battens (K)	4	220 x 18 x 18
small side battens (L)	4	176 x 18 x 18
large lid battens (M)	2	364 x 18 x 18
medium lid battens (N)	2	280 x 18 x 18
small lid battens (O)	2	196 x 18 x 18

All of the above are in pine

part	quantity	L x W x T
large base (P)	1	476 x 376 x 6
medium base (Q)	1	392 x 292 x 6
small base (R)	1	308 x 208 x 6

All of the above are in birch plywood

(finished sizes, given in millimetres)

Whoever said that "less is more" must have been thinking about these boxes. When they are in use as storage – perhaps full of clothes or toys – they can double as side tables, stools or coffee tables. When empty they can be put to similar uses. If you are short of storage space and furniture, these boxes may be the ideal solution.

Design notes

The boxes are made from narrow boards, and are jointed with battens on the inside corners and across the end of each lid in such a way that each box lid locates firmly on four 45° mitres. The box bases are made from thin plywood, which is let into grooves. All three boxes have a finger hole in the lid. The two smaller boxes have finger hole handles in the sides, and the large box has rope handles.

The weathered driftwood finish has been achieved by scouring the grain with a wire brush, and then giving the wood a thin wash of emulsion paint followed by another scouring and a final sanding. A thin coat of Danish oil, followed by a beeswax burnish, completes the process.

Preparing the wood

Inspect the pine boards and make sure that all knots and splits are well away from the edges of each piece. (If possible, place them on the inside faces of the box.) Use the jigsaw to square the wood to length and width. If a fault develops, find another piece of wood. Make sure all the corners are at right angles. Match up the front, back, side, lid and base boards for each box. Pencil-label all faces and edges.

Cutting the grooves

Mount the router on its table and fit the 6 mm groove cutter. Set the router table fence to 12 mm, so the machine will cut a groove 12 mm in from the edge of the wood. Cut a groove along what will be the lower edge of each of the front, back and side boards. Cut to a depth of 3 mm. Repeat the procedure, setting the depth for 6 mm. Making two passes achieves a better finish, and ensures the cutter lasts longer (step 1).

WORKING DRAWINGS AND DETAIL OF THE NESTING STORAGE BOXES
measurements are given in millimetres

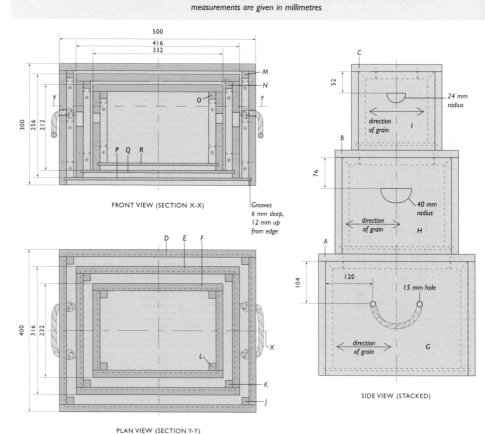

FRONT VIEW (SECTION X-X)

PLAN VIEW (SECTION Y-Y)

SIDE VIEW (STACKED)

Grooves 6 mm deep, 12 mm up from edge

24 mm radius

40 mm radius

15 mm hole

direction of grain

DETAIL OF THE INSIDE OF A BOX
SHOWING THE CORNER CONSTRUCTION

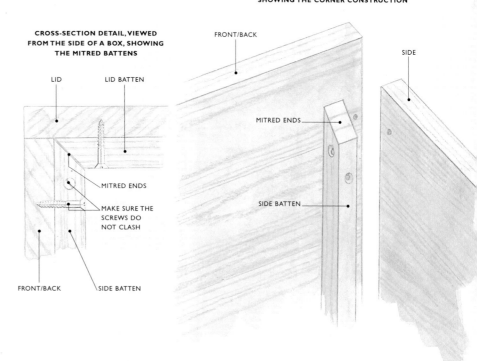

CROSS-SECTION DETAIL, VIEWED FROM THE SIDE OF A BOX, SHOWING THE MITRED BATTENS

LID   LID BATTEN

MITRED ENDS

MAKE SURE THE SCREWS DO NOT CLASH

FRONT/BACK   SIDE BATTEN

FRONT/BACK

MITRED ENDS

SIDE

SIDE BATTEN

Cutting the holes

Mark the position of the various holes and drill them out with the bench drill press and electric drill. Use the 15 mm forstner bit for the rope holes and the pilot holes in the handles, and 38 mm for the lid holes (step 2).

Use the jigsaw to fret out the half-circle shape that makes the handle holes. Work at a steady pace, keeping the saw upright and cutting on the waste side of the drawn line (step 3).

Putting together

Use the mitre saw to cut the top ends of the battens to 45°. Mark the screw positions in the side boards, and drill pilot holes with the electric drill and 5 mm twist bit. Countersink all the holes on the battens so that the screwheads finish flush with the surface. Screw the battens to the inside face of the side boards (step 4).

Blow the dust from the grooves. Slide the plywood base board into the grooved front, back and side boards, and screw the front and back boards to the battens so that the base is contained. Screw the battens across the inside face of the lid boards, and sand everything to a good fit with the power sander. When you have achieved a good overall fit of the lids on the boxes, set to work sanding the corners and edges. Blur the edges so that they are slightly rounded. If an area of soft grain falls away, continue sanding to sculpt the surface (step 5).

Finishing

Fit the rotary wire brush in the electric drill and go over all three boxes systematically scouring out the grain. Pay particular attention to the area around the lid holes, the corner of the lids, and to all areas of end grain. Clean up all the dust and debris, wipe the workpiece with a damp cloth and move to a dust-free area (step 6).

Mix the paint with water to make a thin wash, and coat all surfaces of the boxes and lids, inside and out. Wait until the paint is dry and sand all faces with sandpaper to remove the nibs of grain. Sand in the direction of the grain. Give the boxes a coat of Danish oil or matt varnish. Burnish with beeswax and attach the rope handles.

Pass a piece of rope through the holes in the ends of the large box, and knot the ends on the inside. Make sure that you keep the knots as small as possible (do not use rope that is too stiff to knot properly), so that the smaller boxes do not jam when stacked inside the large box. Finally, when you are happy with the knots, put a dab of PVA glue on them to stop them coming undone.

DESIGN VARIATIONS

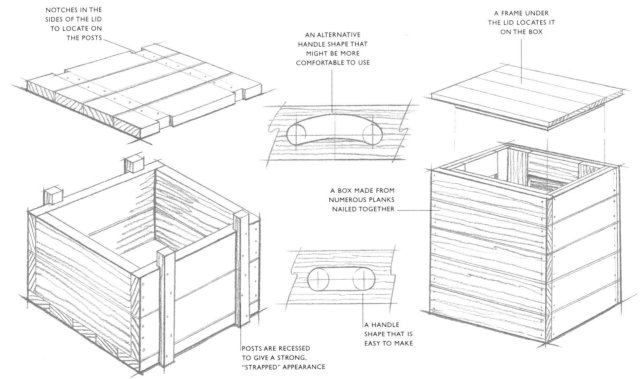

NOTCHES IN THE SIDES OF THE LID TO LOCATE ON THE POSTS

AN ALTERNATIVE HANDLE SHAPE THAT MIGHT BE MORE COMFORTABLE TO USE

A FRAME UNDER THE LID LOCATES IT ON THE BOX

A BOX MADE FROM NUMEROUS PLANKS NAILED TOGETHER

A HANDLE SHAPE THAT IS EASY TO MAKE

POSTS ARE RECESSED TO GIVE A STRONG, "STRAPPED" APPEARANCE

MAKING THE NESTING STORAGE BOXES

1 Routing the grooves
Cut each groove 3 mm deep, then run through again to cut it at 6 mm deep.

2 Drilling the holes
The workpiece should be supported and backed by a piece of waste.

3 Fretting the handle holes
Set the jigsaw blade in the pilot hole, decide on the direction of the cut, then switch on the power and cut just to the waste side of the drawn line.

4 Screwing the battens
Drill pilot holes through the screw positions in the side boards. Screw the battens firmly in place on the inside face of the boards.

5 Putting together
Set the plywood base board in the routed grooves, bring the side, front and back boards together, and screw the front and back boards to the battens.

6 Wire brushing
Work in the direction of the grain, concentrating on corners and edges.

TROUBLESHOOTING

- If you know that all the boards are the correct size, yet find that the base board doesn't fit, make sure the routed groove is not full of dust.

- Don't try to cut costs by using cheap drill bits. Always use forstner bits, which will ensure that all the holes are crisp and clean.

3: KITCHEN BENCH BOX

I f you have a continuing struggle to find a place to put all the family's wellingtons, trainers and walking shoes, this is the answer to all your problems. With plenty of storage space under the flap lid, it has the added advantage of providing a comfortable place to sit, with wide armrests.

TOOLS AND MATERIALS

- workbench, fitted with a vice and holdfast
- square, tape measure, ruler, compass, pencil
- backsaw
- screwdrivers: cross-point and flat
- router, router table, 6 mm groove cutter
- jigsaw
- electric drill, 6 mm counter-bore bit, 6 mm plug cutter
- small spokeshave
- power sander and graded sandpaper
- screws: 50 x 38 mm cross-headed, countersunk screws
- hinges: 2 brass hinges with 13 mm screws to fit
- PVA glue
- Danish oil and beeswax polish
- pine and birch plywood (see cutting list)

CUTTING LIST

part	quantity	L x W x T
back (A)	1	900 x 700 x 18
front (B)	1	900 x 350 x 18
sides (C)	2	352 x 600 x 18
seat (D)	1	860 x 400 x 18
hinge strip (E)	1	864 x 50 x 18
armrests (F)	2	518 x 160 x 18
corner posts (G)	4	400 x 50 x 50
frame pieces (H)	2	252 x 50 x 50
small arm brackets (I)	2	124 x 124 x 50
support blocks (J)	2	500 x 35 x 35
large arm brackets (K)	2	350 x 80 x 18

All of the above are in pine

birch plywood base (L)	1	876 x 364 x 6

(finished sizes, given in millimetres)

This project is inspired by the bench-box seats that used to grace hallways and kitchens back in the 1930s and 40s. The chest form is topped by a hinged seat. The idea is that after a long walk, you slump down on the bench seat and ease off your shoes, then lift up the lid and drop them out of sight until they are next required. Then you can sit back and have a cup of tea, using the armrest to put it on.

Design notes

In essence this is no more than a simple chest, with the side boards being extended to support the armrests and the back board extended to create the backrest. The structure relates to the naïve rural folk woodwork tradition. The whole thing is simply fitted together with glue and screws, just like a crate.

WORKING DRAWINGS AND DETAIL OF THE KITCHEN BENCH BOX *measurements are given in millimetres*

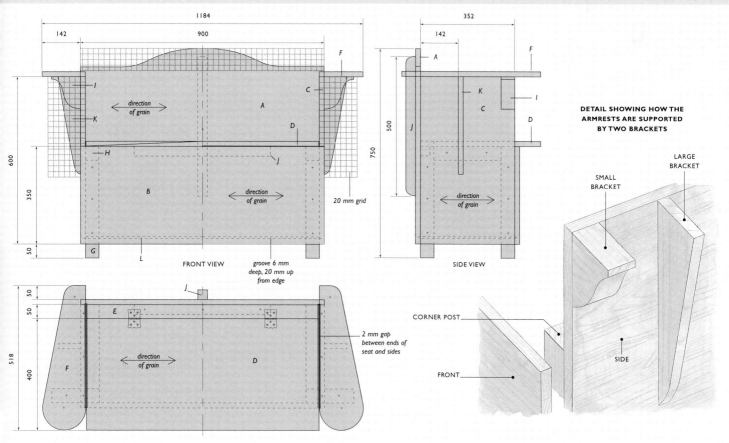

The armrests, support brackets and back boards are shaped and fretted to make them more distinctive. The box structure is both strong and functional. The pine is brushed with Danish oil to enhance its colour and draw attention to the grain.

Preparing the wood

Check the wood and make sure that potentially problematic knots are away from edges. Measure and square the wood to length and width (see pages 10–12). Pencil-label all best faces and top edges, so that you know how the pieces relate to one another.

Cutting and shaping the back

Draw the outline of the back and use the jigsaw to cut out the profile. Set the workpiece in the vice and use the spokeshave to bring the bridge shape to a good finish. Work in the direction of the grain (from the top of the bridge to the end) to avoid cutting into the end grain (step 1).

Fitting the seat and the legs

Attach the router to its table, fit the 6 mm groove cutter and set the router fence to 20 mm. Run a groove 6 mm wide and 6 mm deep, 20 mm up from the bottom edge of the side, front and back boards. The groove runs along the full length of the side and to within 12 mm of the end of the front and back boards (step 2).

Butt the seat to the hinge strip, allowing a 3 mm gap. Screw the hinges to the seat and hinge strip (step 3).

Using the drill and 6 mm counter-bore bit, sink screwholes in the side boards. Screw the sides to the corner posts that make the legs. Make sure that the posts are flush with the edges of the sides. Sink the screws, so they can be plugged later (step 4).

DESIGN VARIATIONS

ALTERNATIVE DOUBLE CURVE BACK SHAPE

ALTERNATIVE SHAPE FOR THE SIDES (WITHOUT ARMRESTS)

ALTERNATIVE PLATEAU AND SLOPING BACK SHAPE

ALTERNATIVE BUN-SHAPED PLATEAU AND RIDGED BACK SHAPE

GENTLY CURVED BACK

A DIFFERENT SHAPE FOR THE ARMREST

S-SHAPED SIDES WITHOUT ARMRESTS

PIERCED HEART MOTIF

BASE RAISED BY CUTTING SHAPE OUT OF THE FRONT BOARD

Use the jigsaw to fret out the armrests according to the working drawing. Work at a steady pace to avoid tearing the wood (step 5).

Putting together

Having drilled all the screwholes with the 6 mm counter-bore bit, screw the front and back boards to the sides and their post legs. The base board, with 50 mm squares removed from each corner, should be contained in the groove (step 6).

Screw the seat support blocks in place on the back and side boards. The top end of the legs and the top face of the support blocks should all be level with the front edge of the front panel. Screw the armrests in place on the side boards. Screw the brackets under the arms so that the structure is braced and the armrests are well supported. Finally, drop the seat board in place (use the power sander to make it fit) and screw the hinge strip to the back support block (step 7).

Finishing

Use the electric drill and 6 mm plug cutter to make plugs for the screwholes. Glue them into the screwholes, and use the power sander to sand the whole box to a smooth, round-edged finish. Clean away the dust and debris before giving all surfaces a thin coat of Danish oil. Finally, rub down the nibs of grain with fine-grade sandpaper and burnish the wood with beeswax.

MAKING THE KITCHEN BENCH BOX

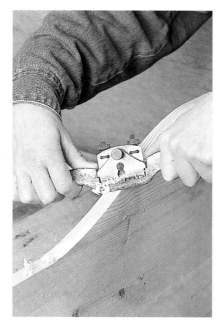

1 Using the spokeshave
Run the spokeshave along the bridge of the back board in the direction of the grain (from high grain to low), to avoid running the blade into the end grain.

2 Routing the grooves
Run a groove 6 mm wide and 6 mm deep, 20 mm up from the bottom edge of all four boards (the two side boards, the front and the back).

3 Hinging the seat
Screw hinges to the hinge strip and seat, leaving 3 mm between the boards.

4 Screwing the sides to the legs
Align the side boards flush with the edge of the leg posts, and screw in place.

5 Cutting the armrests
Make sure that the workpiece is well supported, then switch on the power and run the saw so that the line of cut is just to the waste side of the drawn line.

6 Putting together
Screw the fronts to the sides (plus leg posts) so that the base is contained in the groove. Make sure that the butted ends of the boards are flush and square.

7 Fitting the armrests and seat
Screw the armrests in place on the side boards. Screw the brackets under the arms so that the armrests are well supported. Fix the hinge strip (with the seat board attached) to the back support block.

TROUBLESHOOTING

• If you cannot obtain a plug cutter, for covering up the screwheads, use round-headed brass screws instead of countersunk screws.

4: UNDER-BED BOX

his good-looking, functional box perfectly answers the need for under-bed storage. Instead of all the dusty boxes and saggy plastic bin liners that you have pushed away under your bed, substitute this stylish solution. It will hide away the electric blanket and extra bedding, yet keep them easily accessible.

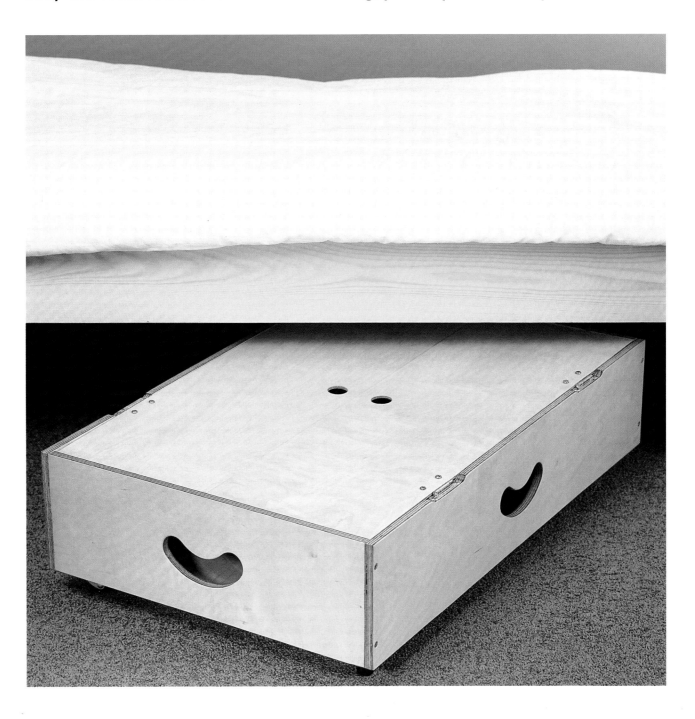

WORKING DRAWINGS AND DETAILS OF THE UNDER-BED BOX *measurements are given in millimetres*

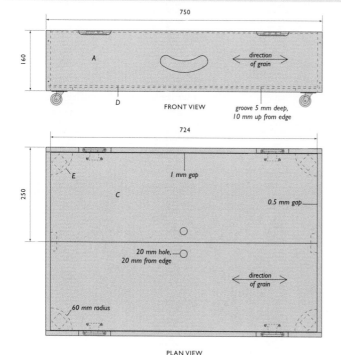

750

160

A

direction
of grain

D

FRONT VIEW

groove 5 mm deep,
10 mm up from edge

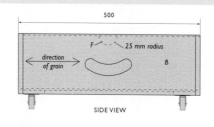

500

F — 25 mm radius

direction
of grain

B

SIDE VIEW

724

250

E

1 mm gap

C

0.5 mm gap

20 mm hole,
20 mm from edge

direction
of grain

60 mm radius

PLAN VIEW

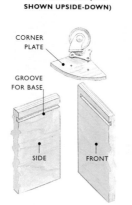

CORNER DETAIL (BOX
SHOWN UPSIDE-DOWN)

CORNER
PLATE

GROOVE
FOR BASE

SIDE

FRONT

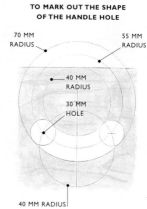

DETAIL SHOWING HOW
TO MARK OUT THE SHAPE
OF THE HANDLE HOLE

70 MM
RADIUS

55 MM
RADIUS

40 MM
RADIUS

30 MM
HOLE

40 MM RADIUS

TOOLS AND MATERIALS

- workbench, fitted with a vice and holdfast
- square, tape measure, ruler, compass, pencil
- backsaw
- screwdrivers: cross-point and flat
- router, router table, 4 mm groove cutter, 16 mm template profile cutter
- jigsaw
- bench drill press and forstner drill bits, 20 mm and 30 mm
- electric drill, small pilot-countersink bit
- power sander and graded sandpaper
- screws: 8 x 32 mm cross-headed, countersunk screws
- hinges: 4 brass "semi-concealed" hinges with nuts and bolts to fit
- wheels: 4 swivel castor wheels with 13 mm screws to fit
- PVA glue
- Danish oil and beeswax polish
- birch plywood and pine (see cutting list)

CUTTING LIST

part	quantity	L x W x T
front/back (A)	2	750 x 160 x 12.5
sides (B)	2	475 x 160 x 12.5
lids (C)	2	724 x 236.5 x 4
base (D)	1	735 x 485 x 4
corner plate (E)	4	60 x 60 x 9.5

All of the above are in birch plywood

pine lid supports (F)	2	50 x 25 x 18

(finished sizes, given in millimetres)

The materials for the box are chosen to be as light as possible, yet the structure is rigid enough to hold its shape. There are "smiley" handle holes on all sides, and swivel wheels on all corners. These enable you to get hold of the box and pull it out from under the bed without doing mischief to the bed, the box or your back. You can fit two boxes under a single bed and four under a double bed.

Design notes

The box is made from seven pieces of plywood – a base board, front, back and side boards, and two hinged lid boards. The front, back and side boards are grooved to take the base board, and their corners are simply butted and screwed so that the edges of the plywood are on full view.

The flap lids are fitted with brass hinges, which are screwed into the top edge of the front and back boards, and bolted through the thickness of the lids. Routed dips allow the hinges to be lowered, so that the lids finish up flush with the top of the sides.

The swivel castor wheels are set on quarter-circle plates of plywood, the idea being that the plates strengthen the corners of the structure and build up the thickness of the base before the wheels are screwed into place. The wheel screws are run through both thicknesses of plywood.

Preparing the wood

Check the seven plywood boards (the front, back and sides, the base and the two lids) to make sure that they are square and crisp-edged. Cut the wood to size (see pages 10–12). Pencil-label the best faces and mark the position of the screwholes, hinges and wheels.

Making the handle holes

Take the four side boards and use a pencil, ruler and compass to set out the shape of the hand holes. Fit the 30 mm forstner bit in the bench drill press and drill out the rounded ends of the holes. Work carefully to avoid tearing the wood (step 1).

Use the jigsaw to finish cutting the shape, linking the holes with two cuts. Work at a steady pace so that you can pull the blade back if it runs off course. You may need to clean up the handle hole with coarse sandpaper wrapped around a dowel (step 2).

Routing and putting together

Fit the router to its table, insert the 4 mm groove cutter, and set the fence to 10 mm. For each front, back and side board, make a groove 4 mm wide and 5 mm deep, 10 mm up from the bottom edge (step 3).

Blow the dust out of the grooves and butt the base together with the other boards so that it is contained in the grooves of the front, back and sides. Use the electric drill and the pilot-countersink bit to drill screwholes in the corners. Fix the corners with countersunk screws (step 4).

Fitting the hardware

Use the jigsaw to cut the shape of the hinge scoop in a piece of waste plywood, making a pattern or jig. Clamp the jig to the inside edge of the front board, aligning it with the top edge, and use the router fitted with the 16 mm template profile cutter to

cut the shape. Repeat this procedure for all four hinge placings (step 5).

Set the box on its base, screw two 25 mm radius half-circle offcuts to the centre of the inside ends of the box to support the lid boards, and fit the two lids in place. Note that there is a gap of 1 mm between the front/back of the box and the hinge side of the lid, and 0.5 mm between the side of the box and the lid. Fix the hinges with screws running into the edge of the routed scoops and bolts through the lid boards. With the bench drill press and 20 mm forstner bit, drill finger holes for opening the lids (step 6).

Turn the box upside-down and glue the wheel plates into the corners. Screw the wheels in place, so that the screws also hold the glued plates in position. Sand the box with the power sander and graded sandpaper, brush on a coat of Danish oil, and finish with beeswax (step 7).

DESIGN VARIATIONS

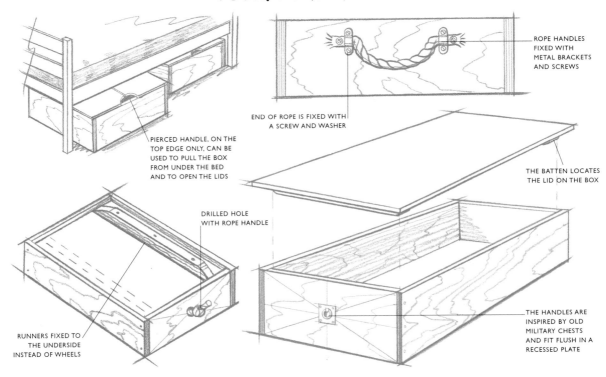

PIERCED HANDLE, ON THE TOP EDGE ONLY, CAN BE USED TO PULL THE BOX FROM UNDER THE BED AND TO OPEN THE LIDS

RUNNERS FIXED TO THE UNDERSIDE INSTEAD OF WHEELS

DRILLED HOLE WITH ROPE HANDLE

ROPE HANDLES FIXED WITH METAL BRACKETS AND SCREWS

END OF ROPE IS FIXED WITH A SCREW AND WASHER

THE BATTEN LOCATES THE LID ON THE BOX

THE HANDLES ARE INSPIRED BY OLD MILITARY CHESTS AND FIT FLUSH IN A RECESSED PLATE

MAKING THE UNDER-BED BOX

1 Drilling the handle holes
Fit the 30 mm forstner bit in the bench drill press, put a piece of waste under the workpiece, and run a hole through at each end of the handle shape.

2 Sawing the handle holes
Support the workpiece, and use the jigsaw to link the two holes with two cuts, so that the piece of waste drops clear. Do this for all the handle holes.

3 Routing the grooves
With the router, cut a 5 mm-deep groove in each side board.

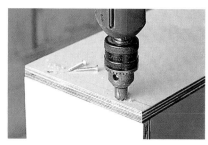

4 Joining front, back and sides
Butt the base and the other boards together, drill and screw.

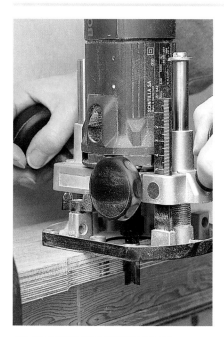

5 Routing the hinge scoop
Clamp the pattern jig to the inside edge of the front board. Fit the router with the 16 mm template profile cutter and cut the scoop.

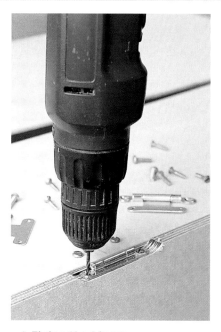

6 Fixing the hinges
Sit the hinges in position – one flap resting on the top edge of the front/back board and the other flap under the lid – and fix with screws and bolts.

7 Fixing the wheels
Glue the wheel plates in position. Screw the wheels on through the plates.

TROUBLESHOOTING

- If the edges of the plywood are damaged after sawing the handles with the jigsaw, you can improve the appearance by routing a profile around the edge of the handles. Use a router and a chamfer or radius cutter with a bearing or guide pin.
- When you buy the castor wheels, choose some that swivel 360°.

5: SMALL PINE CHEST

Grandfather used to have a small chest that he kept close to his chair. It fascinated us – it wasn't big, or made from an exotic wood, and we never did get to open the lid and peek inside, but somehow or other it was special. These are the memories behind the design of our pine chest.

TOOLS AND MATERIALS

- workbench, fitted with a vice and holdfast
- square, tape measure, ruler, pencil
- backsaw
- screwdrivers: cross-point and flat
- router, router table, 6 mm groove cutter, 10 mm radius cutter
- biscuit jointer, 12 number 20 biscuits, biscuit jointer glue bottle
- clamps: 4 sash clamps
- mitre saw
- electric drill with twist bit, sizes to suit the screws
- power sander and graded sandpaper
- pin hammer

- chisel: 20 mm, bevel-edged
- hinges: 2 butt hinges, 50 mm x 18 mm with 16 mm screws
- handles: 2 chest handles with 16 mm screws
- padlock catch with 16 mm screws
- chain: 2 x 300 mm lengths with 4 x 16 mm dome-headed screws with washers
- pins: 20 x 25 mm long
- PVA glue
- Danish oil and beeswax polish
- pine and birch plywood (see cutting list)

CUTTING LIST

part	quantity	L x W x T
lid (A)	1	760 x 440 x 18
front/back (B)	2	700 x 400 x 18
sides (C)	2	364 x 400 x 18
dado rail (including waste)	1	2434 x 70 x 23
All of the above are in pine		
birch plywood base (D)	1	676 x 376 x 6
(finished sizes, given in millimetres)		

The design of our chest is straightforward. It is made from pine boards, with a dado moulding at floor level, a hinged flap lid, and has traditional Victorian black iron handles.

Design notes

The construction of this classic chest has been updated by using biscuit joints rather than dowels, and the base board is let into a slot instead of being nailed against a batten. The boards are arranged so that the front and back boards show end grain on the end view. Traditionally, the dado moulding would have been butted and nailed at the corners, but we have chosen to use mitre joints. We decided that the handles needed to be absolutely simple and functional, so chose black iron lift-and-plate handles screwed to the end boards.

Preparing the wood

Check the wood for possible problems such as splits and knots. Measure and square the wood to length and width (see pages 10–12). Select the face and the top edge of each board to show the best grain. Ensure that knots will be hidden from view. The top edge of the back board needs to be free from knots, as the hinges can then be recessed without difficulty.

WORKING DRAWINGS AND DETAIL OF THE SMALL PINE CHEST *measurements are given in millimetres*

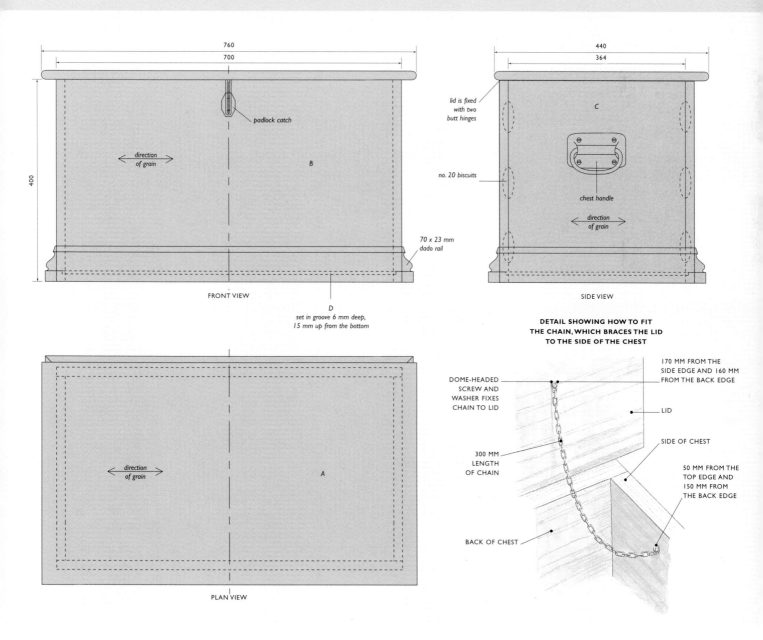

DETAIL SHOWING HOW TO FIT THE CHAIN, WHICH BRACES THE LID TO THE SIDE OF THE CHEST

Making the joints

Use a pencil and ruler to set out the size and position of the groove that runs around the bottom edge of the inside face of all four boards. Set up the router and table with the 6 mm groove cutter, and adjust the fence to 15 mm. Switch on the power and run the boards through to create a groove 6 mm wide, 6 mm deep and 15 mm up from the bottom edge (step 1).

Mark the position of the biscuit centres on the butt joint of the front and side, and back and side. Take one side board and its mating front or back board and clamp them firmly to the bench. Set the biscuit jointer so that the slot is centred within the thickness of the board, then have a trial run on some scrap wood of the same thickness. Then plunge the slots in the side board (step 2).

With the two boards still clamped down in the same position, flip the biscuit jointer over so that the cutter is on target for cutting the slots on the front board. Plunge it down and make the cuts (step 3).

Putting together

Have a trial run just to make sure that the slots are well placed, then use the special glue bottle to smear glue in the slots. Spread glue over the end grain of the side boards and biscuits. Slide the base board into place and push the joints together. Put the clamps in position across the width of the box, inserting pieces of scrap wood between the clamp and the wood to prevent any damage to the surface of the box (step 4).

Wait for the glue to cure, then remove the clamps and sand the corners of the box to a good finish with the power sander and graded sandpaper. Cut the dado moulding on

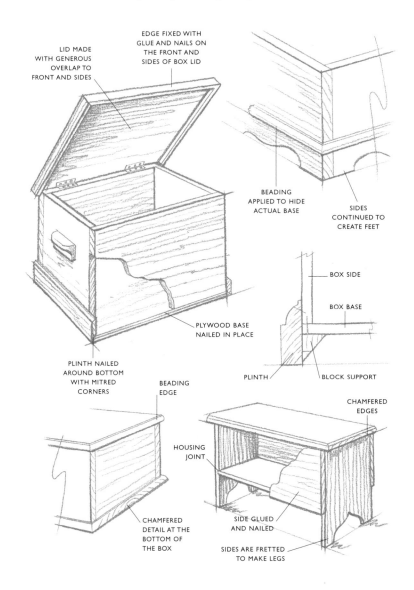

DESIGN VARIATIONS

LID MADE WITH GENEROUS OVERLAP TO FRONT AND SIDES

EDGE FIXED WITH GLUE AND NAILS ON THE FRONT AND SIDES OF BOX LID

BEADING APPLIED TO HIDE ACTUAL BASE

SIDES CONTINUED TO CREATE FEET

PLYWOOD BASE NAILED IN PLACE

PLINTH NAILED AROUND BOTTOM WITH MITRED CORNERS

BOX SIDE

BOX BASE

PLINTH

BLOCK SUPPORT

BEADING EDGE

CHAMFERED EDGES

HOUSING JOINT

CHAMFERED DETAIL AT THE BOTTOM OF THE BOX

SIDE GLUED AND NAILED

SIDES ARE FRETTED TO MAKE LEGS

the mitre saw, smear glue on the sawn face, and glue and pin it in place around the base of the box (step 5).

Making and fitting the lid

To shape the lid, fit the router with the 10 mm radius cutter. Make three passes for each right-angled edge – one to cut off the corner, one to remove the bulk of the waste and one to achieve the finished rounded profile. Repeat the same sequence for the other side of the lid (step 6).

Chop hinge recesses on the top edge of the back board and the underside of the lid with the chisel. Drill pilot holes for the screws and screw the hinges in place. Fit the two chains with the dome-headed screws and washers, and screw the padlock catch and the handles into position (step 7).

Sand the chest with the power sander, and finish with fine-grade sandpaper. Finally, brush over all the surfaces with Danish oil. Let it dry and burnish with beeswax.

MAKING THE SMALL PINE CHEST

Routing the base groove
Aim to complete the 6 mm-deep groove in three passes.

2 **Cutting slots in the sides**
Work with the biscuit jointer flat on scrap board supporting the workpiece.

3 **Cutting slots in the front**
Set the biscuit jointer upright so that it is sitting squarely over the edge of the board, determine where you want the cuts to be made, then make the cut.

4 **Gluing and clamping**
Fill the slots with glue, smear glue on the end grain, set the biscuits in place and push the boards together. Clamp across the box.

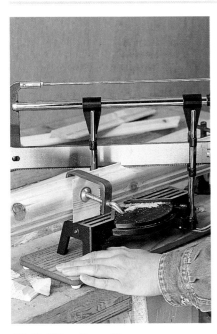

5 **Cutting the mitres**
Use a pencil, ruler and square to establish the length of the moulding and position of the mitre. Put the workpiece in the mitre saw, clamp and cut.

6 **Routing the lid profile**
Push the workpiece through swiftly to remove the corner, once more to remove the bulk of the waste and a final pass to make the rounded profile.

7 **Fitting the hinges**
Chisel a recess for the hinge plate, so it sits flush with the surface.

TROUBLESHOOTING

- Don't attempt to cut grooves with a single, deep thrust – it is much better to take three or more passes to achieve the final depth.

- Don't try to cut costs by doing without the biscuit glue bottle. Make sure that you clean out the slots prior to gluing.

6: FOLK ART HALLWAY BOX

T his project is reminiscent of English pipe boxes, Pennsylvanian German candle boxes, and a whole host of other little traditional boxes. Hung on the wall in the hallway, the box is the perfect place to store everything from car keys and dog leads to spare shoelaces and loose change.

WORKING DRAWINGS AND DETAIL OF THE FOLK ART HALLWAY BOX
measurements are given in millimetres

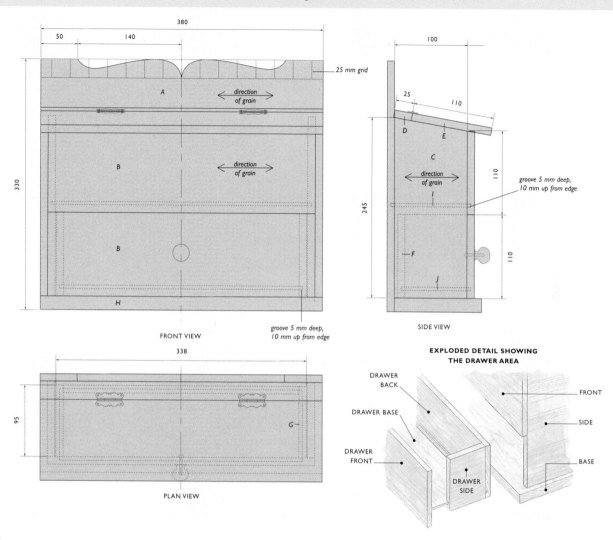

FRONT VIEW

SIDE VIEW

PLAN VIEW

EXPLODED DETAIL SHOWING
THE DRAWER AREA

DRAWER BACK
DRAWER BASE
DRAWER FRONT
DRAWER SIDE
FRONT
SIDE
BASE

25 mm grid
direction of grain
groove 5 mm deep, 10 mm up from edge

TOOLS AND MATERIALS

- workbench, fitted with a vice and holdfast
- square, tape measure, ruler, pencil, tracing paper
- backsaw
- router, router table, 4 mm groove cutter
- scroll saw
- pin hammer
- long-nose pliers
- small iron block

- electric drill and 8 mm drill bit
- power sander and graded sandpaper
- pins: 25 x 20 mm long
- hinges: 2 decorative brass hinges with 9 mm brass dome-headed pins to fit
- acrylic paint in brick red, paintbrush
- PVA glue
- Danish oil and beeswax polish
- pine and birch plywood (see cutting list)

CUTTING LIST

part	quantity	L x W x T
back (A)	1	380 x 330 x 10
front/drawer front (B)	2	360 x 110 x 10
sides (C)	2	100 x 245 x 10
hinge strip (D)	1	380 x 25 x 10
lid (E)	1	380 x 110 x 10
drawer back (F)	1	318 x 110 x 10
drawer sides (G)	2	95 x 110 x 10
base (H)	1	380 x 120 x 18

All of the above are in pine

platform (I)	1	350 x 110 x 4
drawer base (J)	1	328 x 95 x 4

All of the above are in birch plywood

(finished sizes, given in millimetres)

This beautiful box perfectly captures the spirit of the folk art tradition. If you travelled back in time one hundred years and looked in a cottage in the Scottish highlands, or a farmhouse in Sweden, or a homestead in the American West, you would see boxes like this on the walls. Designed for holding items such as candles, tobacco, salt and cutlery, they were often made by the man of the house as a love token or Christmas gift.

Design notes

The box is made from thirteen pieces. For the main structure there is a back board, two side boards and a base board, the lid and its accompanying hinge strip, a platform, and a front board above the drawer. The other pieces are used for making the drawer.

The back board has a cyma curve profile, the lid hinges back to reveal a useful storage space, and the drawer front runs the full width of the back board. The structure is faithful to the spirit of the folk art tradition, in that the whole box is fitted together with pins – there are no joints at all, just pins. The surfaces are finished by colour-washing and waxing.

Preparing the wood

Inspect the wood for problems. Check to make sure that the plywood has no cavities or stains, and that the pine has no awkwardly placed knots and splits that run into the end grain. Use the backsaw and scroll saw to square the boards to length and width.

Fretting and routing

Trace and press-transfer the shape of the cyma curve on the back board. Fit and re-tension a new blade on the scroll saw. Switch on the power and run the workpiece forward so that the blade is presented with the line of cut. Fret out the cyma curve. Be sure to run the cut a little to the waste side of the drawn line (step 1).

Attach the router to its table, fit the 4 mm groove cutter, and set the fence to 10 mm. Run a groove 5 mm deep and 10 mm up from the bottom edge, on the inside face of the front board, and on the inside face of all the drawer components. Re-run the procedure 120 mm up on the inside faces of the side boards (set the fence to 120 mm), and 140 mm up on the inside face of the back board (set the fence to 140 mm).

Putting together

Sand all the wood to a smooth finish with the power sander and fine-grade sandpaper (step 2).

Glue and pin the basic carcass together, nailing through the back and front boards and into the edges of the side boards. The plywood above-drawer platform board is contained in the groove (step 3).

Make the drawer by nailing through the sides into the back. Slide the plywood base board into the groove on the inside face of the drawer front. Pin the drawer front in place on the sides. The heads of the pins will be visible on the drawer front. Use the long-nose pliers to hold and manoeuvre the pins (step 4).

Hinging the lid strip and finishing

Set the hinge strip alongside the lid, bridge them with the brass hinges, and fix with the brass pins. Use the pin hammer and iron block to clench the points of the pins on the inside face of the lid. Finally, pin the hinge strip in place on the end boards (step 5).

Give the box a thin wash of brick red acrylic paint. When the paint is completely dry, rub the wood to a smooth finish with the power sander and graded sandpaper. Lastly, give all the surfaces a thin coat of Danish oil, wait until the oil is dry and burnish with beeswax.

DESIGN VARIATIONS

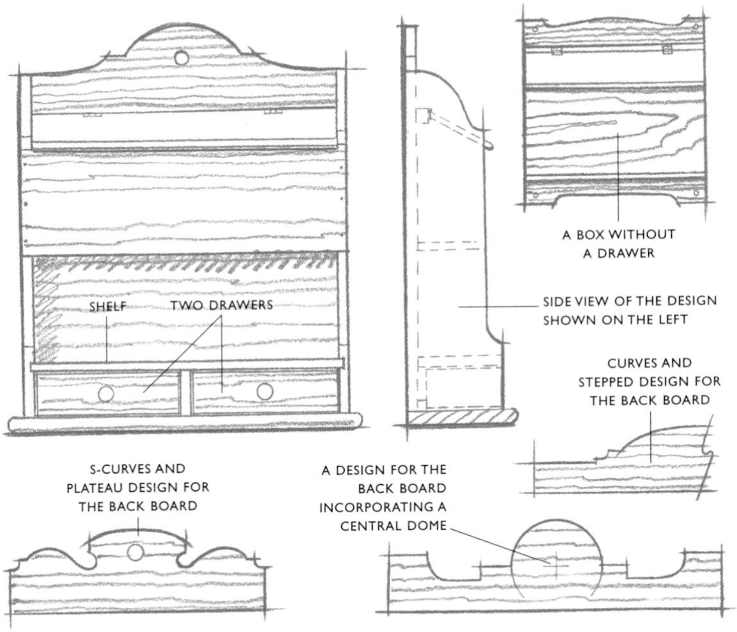

SHELF   TWO DRAWERS

S-CURVES AND PLATEAU DESIGN FOR THE BACK BOARD

A DESIGN FOR THE BACK BOARD INCORPORATING A CENTRAL DOME

A BOX WITHOUT A DRAWER

SIDE VIEW OF THE DESIGN SHOWN ON THE LEFT

CURVES AND STEPPED DESIGN FOR THE BACK BOARD

MAKING THE FOLK ART HALLWAY BOX

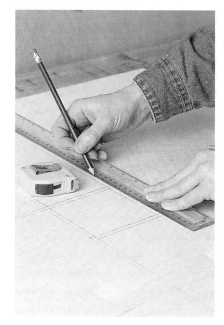

1 Using the scroll saw
Trace the cyma curve on the back board. Run a starter cut straight down into the centre of the cyma. Follow with cuts in from the ends of the board.

2 Sanding
Use the power sander to sand the boards to a smooth finish. Wrap a piece of fine-grade sandpaper around a dowel, and use this to clean up the shape of the back. Aim for a slightly round-edged finish, with the edges of the curves being nicely blurred.

5 Fixing the hinge strip
Fix with brass pins, then turn over and clench the points of the pins.

TROUBLESHOOTING

- If you are at all worried about the wood splitting when you drive in the pins, drill pilot holes first.
- When you are sanding, make sure that you blur all the corners and edges, so that the finished box achieves a timeworn appearance.

3 Nailing and gluing the carcass
Have a trial fitting to make sure that all the component parts come together, and then dribble a bead of glue on mating faces and fix with pins.

4 Nailing and gluing the drawer
Set the sides in place and glue and nail through to the back board. Slide the base board in the groove on the inside face of the drawer front.

7: COFFEE TABLE WITH BASKETS

If you like pieces of furniture that perform more than a single task, this project will appeal to you. It's a low coffee table with useful drawers, perfect for a Sunday morning's relaxation with the newspapers, drinking coffee – when you've finished reading, you simply pop the papers out of sight in the baskets.

TOOLS AND MATERIALS

- workbench, fitted with a vice and holdfast
- square, tape measure, ruler, compass, pencil
- backsaw
- screwdrivers: cross-point and flat
- router, 6 mm groove cutter
- batten for the guide strip: 600 mm long, 20 mm wide, 10 mm deep
- jigsaw
- clamps: 2 sash clamps
- power sander and graded sandpaper
- chisel
- screws: 2 x 25 mm countersunk screws for fixing guide strip in place
- wheels: 4 castor wheels with 13 mm screws to fit
- scraper
- baskets: 4 woven willow baskets, 410 x 300 x 150 mm
- PVA glue
- Danish oil and beeswax polish
- birch plywood (see cutting list)

CUTTING LIST

part	quantity	L x W x T
tabletop (A)	1	870 x 870 x 19
base (B)	1	750 x 750 x 19
divisions (C)	4	420 x 190 x 6

All of the above are in birch plywood

(finished sizes, given in millimetres)

This project has been designed for the beginner who is keen to make an impressive piece of furniture with some storage facility, yet who is a bit worried about the thought of making drawers, particularly if they involve dovetail joints, which are more time-consuming. Ready-made baskets are used instead of drawers, and when they are in place, the table appears to be made almost entirely of woven willow. This table would look especially good in a modern, Swedish-style room, alongside a couple of traditional rattan or wicker chairs.

Design notes

The shape and size of this table have been designed so that they relate to the size of the woven baskets it contains. However, because you may not be able to obtain baskets in the exact sizes that we have specified, it is preferable to buy the baskets first and then adjust the dimensions of the finished table to fit.

Apart from the four woven baskets, the project is made from six plywood boards – the tabletop, the base, and four dividing boards. The design is clever in that the vertical dividing boards (seen on the side elevations) are set together and housed in grooves, creating a tough and rigid honeycomb structure that is easily strong enough to sit on. The table stands on four swivel wheels that allow it to be moved around.

Preparing the wood

Take the six pieces of plywood – the tabletop and base boards and the four dividing panels – and make sure that they are free from faults. Cut the wood to size with the jigsaw. Mark the best face of the tabletop and the top face of the base board. If you are working to sizes that are different to those on the materials list, double-check that the baskets are appropriate for the table's dimensions.

WORKING DRAWINGS AND DETAIL OF THE COFFEE TABLE WITH BASKETS
measurements are given in millimetres

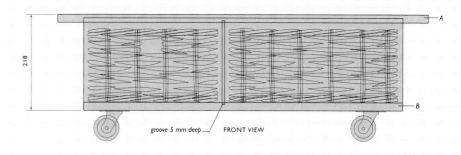

groove 5 mm deep   FRONT VIEW

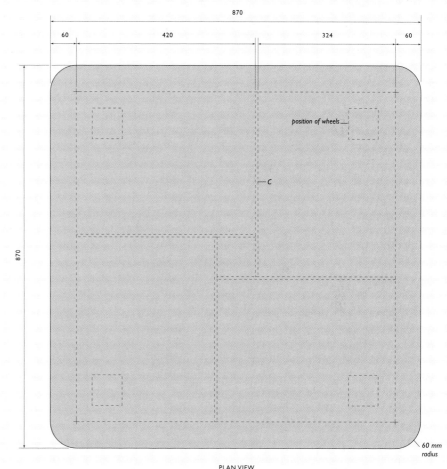

PLAN VIEW

DETAIL OF THE CENTRE OF THE TABLE

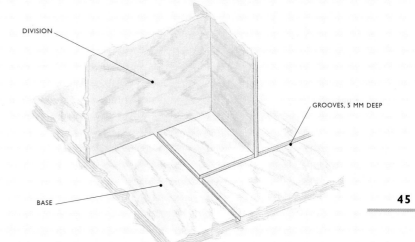

DIVISION

GROOVES, 5 MM DEEP

BASE

45

Routing grooves
and cutting corners

Mark out the position and extent of the grooves on the underside of the tabletop and the top face of the base board. Make sure that from board to board, the position of the grooves is the mirror image reversed: when the two boards are set together, the drawn lines should be in contact (like putting your hands together) (step 1).

Fit the 6 mm groove cutter in the router. Screw the guide strip parallel and square to a marked groove with the 25 mm countersunk screws, so the router bit is on target. Rout out the four grooves on each board to a depth of 5 mm. Work at a steady pace to avoid stressing the router or burning the wood. Make sure that the angle between the guide strip and the board is free from dust (step 2).

Set the compass to a radius of 60 mm and mark out the curves on the corners of the tabletop. Cut them with the jigsaw. Make sure that the sole of the jigsaw is sitting level on the board, so that the sawn edge is at right angles to the face (step 3).

Putting together

Brush the dust from the grooves and have a trial fit of the dividing panels. Dribble glue in the grooves (on both the base board and the tabletop) and slide the dividing panels into place in the base board. Put the tabletop in position and clamp up. Remember to put pieces of scrap wood between the clamp heads and the workpiece. When the glue has set, remove the clamps and very carefully use a chisel and sandpaper to remove stray blobs of dry glue (step 4).

Finally, mark in the positions of the wheels on the base board and drill pilot holes for the screws.

Fitting the wheels and finishing

Screw the wheels to the underside of the base board. If your plywood has deep sanding marks running across the grain (this is a common flaw due to the manufacturing process), use a scraper to remove them before sanding. Sand the table to a smooth finish with the power sander. Clear up the dust and debris and brush on a thin coat of Danish oil. Rub down all the surfaces with the graded sandpaper to remove the nibs of grain, and burnish with beeswax polish. Slide the baskets into position. If you have bought inexpensive baskets that were made quickly with little regard for finish, wipe them over with white spirit and give them a coat of matt varnish (step 5).

DESIGN VARIATIONS

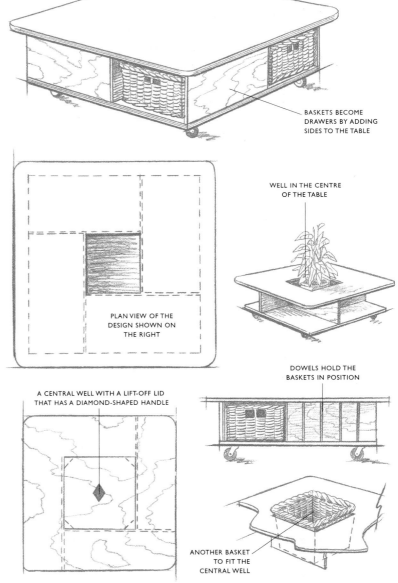

BASKETS BECOME DRAWERS BY ADDING SIDES TO THE TABLE

PLAN VIEW OF THE DESIGN SHOWN ON THE RIGHT

A CENTRAL WELL WITH A LIFT-OFF LID THAT HAS A DIAMOND-SHAPED HANDLE

WELL IN THE CENTRE OF THE TABLE

DOWELS HOLD THE BASKETS IN POSITION

ANOTHER BASKET TO FIT THE CENTRAL WELL

MAKING THE COFFEE TABLE

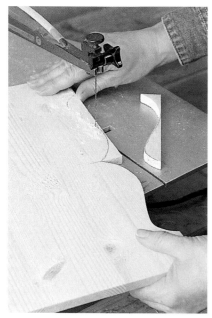

Marking out the grooves

Establish the centre of the tabletop and base board, and set out the grooves. From board to board, the layout of the grooves is mirror image reversed.

2 Routing the grooves

Screw a guide strip parallel and square to a marked groove so the router bit is on target. Rout out four grooves on each board, making them 5 mm deep.

3 Cutting the corners

Cut out the corner curves on the tabletop with the jigsaw. Work slowly, making sure that the line of cut is a little to the waste side of the drawn line.

5 Fixing the wheels

Screw the four wheels in position and check that they are turning freely.

TROUBLESHOOTING

• The easiest mistake to make when reversing the grooves from one board to another is not to make them a mirror image.

• Don't try to cut costs by using Malaysian plywood, because it is soft and spongy. Use American or European birch plywood.

4 Putting together

Brush the dust from the grooves. Dribble glue in the grooves in the base board and tabletop, and on the ends of the dividing panels. Slide the panels in place in the base board, and sit the tabletop in position. Clamp up, putting pieces of scrap wood between the clamps and the workpiece. Clean up any dribbles of glue.

8: MARQUETRY JEWELLERY BOX

This project was sparked off by the stunning work of the artist **Gustav Klimt.** Our jewellery box weaves together squares of wood, and although it may appear complex, the techniques for making it are relatively simple. The project is well within the scope of a keen beginner.

CUTTING LIST

part	quantity	L x W x T
top of lid/base of box (A)	2	195 x 150 x 6
front/back of lid (B)	2	195 x 24 x 6
front/back of box (C)	2	195 x 99 x 6
sides of lid (D)	2	138 x 24 x 6
sides of base (E)	2	138 x 99 x 6
base of tray (F)	1	175 x 130 x 4
All of the above are in birch plywood		
support posts in box (G)	4	68 x 6 x 6
All of the above are in pine		
long tray sides (H)	2	175 x 35 x 6
short tray sides (I)	2	136 x 35 x 6
long tray divisions (J)	2	83.5 x 20 x 4
short tray divisions (K)	2	61 x 20 x 4
central tray post (L)	1	35 x 10 x 10
All of the above are in maple		
(finished sizes, given in millimetres)		

TOOLS AND MATERIALS

- workbench, fitted with a vice and holdfast
- square, tape measure, ruler, pencil
- backsaw
- screwdrivers: cross-point and flat
- router, router table, 4 mm groove cutter, 10 mm straight cutter
- craft knife and steel rule
- 0.6 mm veneer: 205 x 160 mm pieces of pink cherry, grey-stained sycamore and plain sycamore
- whittling knife
- pin hammer and pliers
- clamps: 4 G-clamps

- electric iron
- power sander and graded sandpaper
- steel pins: 40 x 20 mm
- hinges: 2 decorative brass hinges with brass pins to fit
- paper tape: lick-and-stick brown gummed tape
- acrylic paint in matt black, 25 mm paintbrush
- PVA glue
- Danish oil and beeswax polish
- small brass flip catch with screws to fit
- birch plywood, pine and maple (see cutting list)

Gustav Klimt's painting, *The Kiss*, shows two lovers, with the man dressed in a long, flowing golden robe made from hundreds of shimmering coloured squares. The idea of building a pattern from marquetry squares comes from an inlay technique known as parquetry. In essence, little strips of coloured veneer are set side by side and glued, and then cut with a craft knife and reset in such a way that the pattern becomes smaller and more involved. The technique is similar to patchwork, where a pattern is constructed from tessellating shapes.

WORKING DRAWINGS AND DETAILS OF THE MARQUETRY JEWELLERY BOX *measurements are given in millimetres*

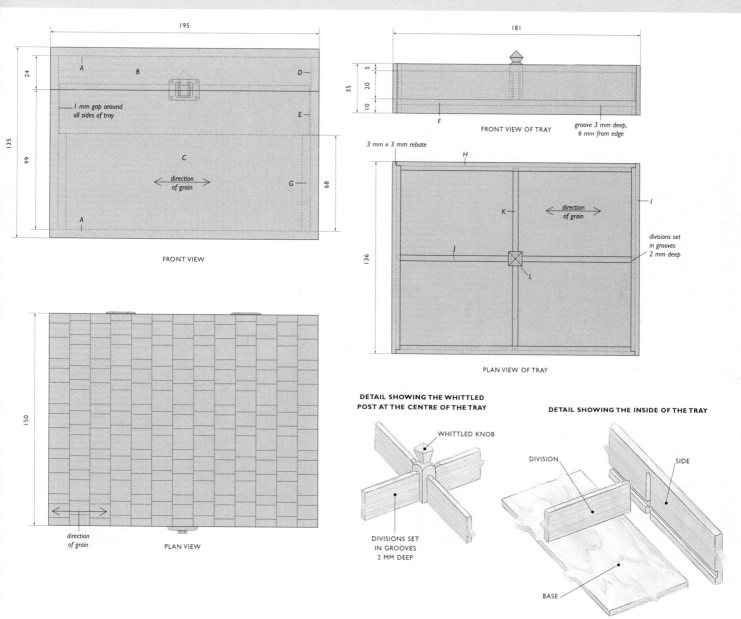

FRONT VIEW

PLAN VIEW

direction of grain

FRONT VIEW OF TRAY

groove 3 mm deep, 6 mm from edge

3 mm x 3 mm rebate

direction of grain

divisions set in grooves 2 mm deep

PLAN VIEW OF TRAY

DETAIL SHOWING THE WHITTLED POST AT THE CENTRE OF THE TRAY

WHITTLED KNOB

DIVISIONS SET IN GROOVES 2 MM DEEP

DETAIL SHOWING THE INSIDE OF THE TRAY

DIVISION

SIDE

BASE

Design notes

The box structure is made up from 24 components. The lower half of the box has a base board, front, back and sides; the lid has a top board, front, back and sides. There is an inside tray with four sides, a base, four divisions and a post at the centre. Four posts support the tray. The basic structure of the box is butted and pinned; the tray is rebated and housed.

The top of the central post is whittled to make a little knob. The outer box is covered with decorative veneers.

Preparing the wood

Measure and cut the wood to length and width (see pages 10–12). Take the plywood, pine and maple, and the three sheets of veneer (grey-stained sycamore, pink cherry and plain or white sycamore), and check to make sure that the sizes are correct and the veneers are free from splits and holes. Pencil-label all the parts so that you know how they relate to each other.

Making the box

Set the pieces of plywood together for the lid and the box base. For the lid, the sides are captured between the front, back and top board; for the box base, the sides are captured between the front, back and base board. All joints are glued and pinned. The pins are held and manoeuvred with pliers. Glue the support posts into the corners of the box (step 1).

Cutting the veneers

Use the craft knife and steel rule to cut the primary strips of veneer. Make the grey sycamore strips 7 mm wide, 10 mm for the pink cherry, and 15 mm for the white sycamore (step 2).

Assemble the strips side by side, in random order, and fix them together with paper tape. Cover the whole arrangement with paper tape. This is removed at a later stage (step 3).

Cut across the taped assembly to make 15 mm-wide secondary strips (step 4).

Reassemble the secondary strips in a staggered pattern, flipping some strips round, end to end. Fix with paper tape (step 5).

Ironing on the veneers

Brush PVA glue over the top of the box and on the side of the strip assembly that is not covered by paper tape, and let it dry. Set the veneers in place on the box, with the paper face uppermost, and use a hot iron to press them in place (step 6).

Sand all sides of the box with the power sander, cutting through the tape to reveal the underlying veneer. Use the finest grade of abrasive and work with caution so you do not damage the veneer (step 7).

Building the tray and finishing

Gather all the component parts for the tray. With the router and 10 mm straight cutter, cut rebates in the corners of the side strips. Attach the router to its table and fit the 4 mm groove cutter. Set the fence to

make a cut 6 mm from the edge. Cut grooves in the sides for the base board (3 mm deep) and the dividing strips (2 mm deep), and a groove in the central post (2 mm deep). All the grooves are 4 mm wide. Fold sandpaper around a ruler and carefully smooth away all the rough edges.

Whittle the central post to make a lifting knob. Assemble the tray, capturing the base board and dividing strips in grooves, and glue and clamp

together. Paint the interior and the edges of the veneered box with matt black paint. Hinge the lid to the box base. Give the whole box a thin coat of Danish oil. Rub down with the power sander and fine-grade sandpaper. Burnish with beeswax polish. Finally, rework with sandpaper to cut back any high spots, rewax and repeat the burnishing. Use a clean, lint-free cotton cloth to create a high-sheen finish. Fit the flip catch (step 8).

DESIGN VARIATIONS

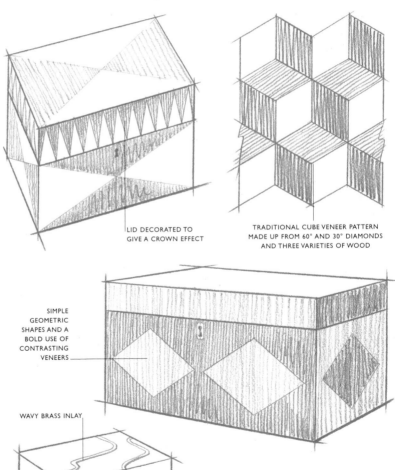

LID DECORATED TO GIVE A CROWN EFFECT

TRADITIONAL CUBE VENEER PATTERN MADE UP FROM 60° AND 30° DIAMONDS AND THREE VARIETIES OF WOOD

SIMPLE GEOMETRIC SHAPES AND A BOLD USE OF CONTRASTING VENEERS

WAVY BRASS INLAY

SMALL BUN FEET

A LONGER SHAPED BOX WITH TWO REMOVABLE TRAYS SIDE BY SIDE

MAKING THE MARQUETRY JEWELLERY BOX

Putting the box together
With the sides captured between the front and back, butt joint the corners.

2 **Cutting the primary strips**
Use the steel rule and craft knife to cut the sheets of veneer into strips.

3 **Assembling the primary strips**
Assemble the primary strips side by side in random order. Fix them in place with tabs of paper tape, and then cover the whole arrangement with paper tape.

4 **Cutting the secondary strips**
Re-run the cutting procedure, but this time cut across the assembly to make a number of secondary strips, all 15 mm wide.

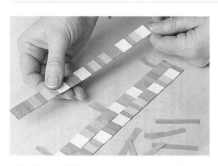

5 **Assembling secondary strips**
Arrange in a staggered pattern, with some strips turned round end to end.

6 **Ironing on the veneer**
Set the veneers in place on the box and use a hot iron to fix them in place.

7 **Sanding the veneer**
Hold the lid firmly and use a power sander and coarse abrasive to remove all the gummed tape. Complete the sanding with very fine-grade abrasive.

8 **Making the tray**
Use a router table to cut the corner rebates, base grooves and housings.

TROUBLESHOOTING

• Do not use masking tape on the veneers or it will strip off the finish. You must use gummed brown paper tape that you dampen with water.

• Use scraps of veneer to experiment with the ironing, so that you can correctly judge the heat setting and the length of contact required.

9: MEMPHIS PENCIL BOX

The famous Canary Wharf tower in London's Docklands is not to everyone's architectural taste, but seeing it glinting starkly against the skyline, it reminded us of a giant pencil box! That was the starting point for this project. If you enjoy precise woodwork, you can make a unique gift.

TOOLS AND MATERIALS

- workbench, fitted with a vice and holdfast
- square, tape measure, ruler, pencil, tracing paper
- backsaw
- screwdrivers: cross-point and flat
- router, router table, 10 mm straight cutter, 45° mitre cutter
- scroll saw
- mitre saw
- penknife
- bench drill press, 12 mm forstner bit, 5 mm twist bit, 12 mm twist bit
- clamps: 2 G-clamps
- power sander and graded sandpaper
- acrylic paint in colour to suit, small paintbrush
- PVA glue
- Danish oil and beeswax polish
- cherry and maple (see cutting list)

CUTTING LIST

part	quantity	L x W x T
cherry sides (A)	4	213 x 70 x 6
maple core block (B)	1	120 x 58 x 58
maple nose block (C)	1	70 x 70 x 70

(finished sizes, given in millimetres)

While the Canary Wharf tower was the impetus for the pencil box, its design is also a tongue-in-cheek look at the so-called post-modernist Memphis style that peaked in Milan in 1982 – hence the project name. Although a little kitsch, the design is beautifully functional – perfect for an executive's desk. It is so interesting to touch, including the way the lid lifts to reveal the pencils, that it is arguably an art object in its own right, rather like a piece of sculpture.

Design notes

The box is made from six component parts – the four cherry side boards, the maple core block, and the maple nose block. The core block is drilled to take the pencils, the nose block is rebated so that it fits like a lid, and the side boards are mitred so that they fit snugly around the core block.

The box stands on four round feet, whittled with a penknife. The ball shape extends into a dowel which pushes into the base. The making of the box is straightforward – almost easy – thanks to the scroll saw, which is fitted with a fine blade.

Preparing the wood

Saw and plane the wood to size (see pages 10–12). Take the four cherry side panels and the maple core and nose blocks and check that the sizes are correct and the wood is free from awkwardly placed knots and splits, especially on the side panels.

Drilling holes

Mark the centres of the nine holes on the core block. Fit the 12 mm twist bit in the bench drill press, set the depth gauge to stop about 7 mm short of the bottom of the block, and then bore the holes (step 1).

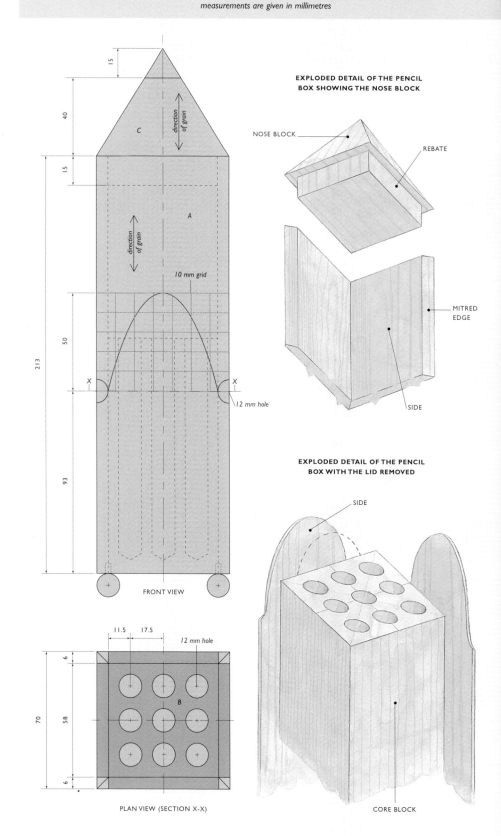

WORKING DRAWINGS AND DETAILS OF THE MEMPHIS PENCIL BOX
measurements are given in millimetres

EXPLODED DETAIL OF THE PENCIL BOX SHOWING THE NOSE BLOCK

NOSE BLOCK

REBATE

MITRED EDGE

SIDE

EXPLODED DETAIL OF THE PENCIL BOX WITH THE LID REMOVED

SIDE

CORE BLOCK

15
40
15
C
direction of grain
A
direction of grain
50
93
213
10 mm grid
X   X
12 mm hole
FRONT VIEW

11.5   17.5
12 mm hole
6
58
70
6
B
PLAN VIEW (SECTION X-X)

Clamp a pair of side panels together side by side. Put the 12 mm forstner bit in the drill press and run a hole where the mating edges meet, so that each panel has a half-hole. Repeat for the other sides (step 2).

Making the side panels

Attach the router to its table and fit the 45° mitre cutter. Set the fence to match the thickness of the wood you are mitring. The wood is not a uniform thickness, so the fence has to be adjusted by trial and error, so that the two edges being mitred fit together to make a 90° corner. Have a trial run on some scrap of the same thickness as the side panels, then run mitres on the long edges of all four panels. Check the fit around the core (step 3).

Trace the curved profile from your master design and press-transfer it to the best face of each panel. Fret out the panels on the scroll saw (step 4).

Making the nose block

Fix the router to its table and fit the 10 mm straight cutter. Set the fence to 15 mm. Switch on the power and run a rebate around the base of the nose block. Make it 6 mm deep and 15 mm up from the bottom. Do this on all four sides of the block (step 5).

Use the mitre saw to cut the block into shape. Cut from the bottom to the centre line, on each side of the block, making a pyramid with a rebate around the base (step 6).

Putting together and finishing

Sand all the component parts to a smooth finish with the power sander and sandpaper. Glue the bottom side panels around the core block, and the top side panels around the nose block (make sure that when the lid is in place, the panels are correctly mated up), and then clamp up. When you are testing the lid for fit, be careful to avoid getting glue on the edges. Use a damp cloth to wipe away excess glue, making especially sure that there is none on the drilled face of the core block to spoil the finish (step 7).

Whittle four ball feet from offcuts with the penknife. The ball shape needs to extend into a dowel (7 mm long and 5 mm in diameter) so that each foot can be glued into a hole in the base. Drill four 5 mm holes in the base and glue the feet in place.

Cut a V-section groove around the nose block with the penknife and ruler. This forms the pencil point detail. Paint the nose block and ball feet with acrylic paint, seal with a coat of Danish oil and rub down with sandpaper to remove the nibs of grain. Repeat the oiling and the rubbing down until you achieve a supersmooth finish. Finally, wipe the wood with a little white spirit on a soft cloth and burnish it with beeswax.

DESIGN VARIATIONS

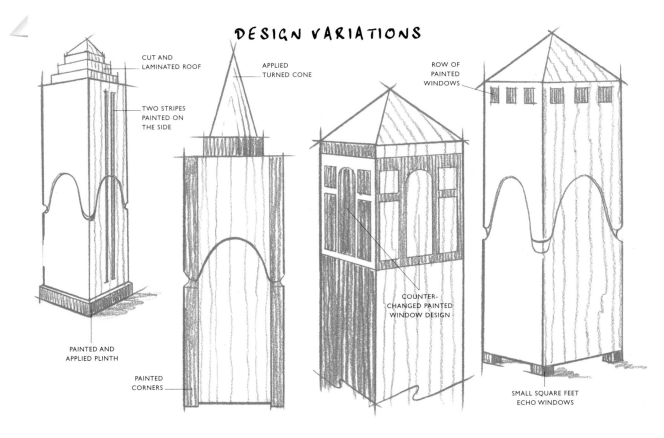

CUT AND
LAMINATED ROOF

TWO STRIPES
PAINTED ON
THE SIDE

PAINTED AND
APPLIED PLINTH

PAINTED
CORNERS

APPLIED
TURNED CONE

ROW OF
PAINTED
WINDOWS

COUNTER-
CHANGED PAINTED
WINDOW DESIGN

SMALL SQUARE FEET
ECHO WINDOWS

MAKING THE MEMPHIS PENCIL BOX

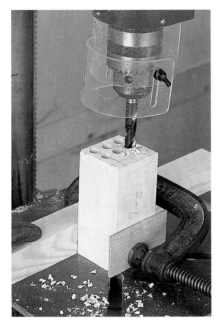

Drilling the core block
Fit the 12 mm twist bit in the drill press, set the depth gauge to stop about 7 mm short of the bottom of the block, then bore out the pattern of nine holes.

2 **Drilling the side panels**
Clamp a pair of side panels together and drill a half-hole in the sides.

3 **Routing the panel mitres**
With the 45° cutter, run mitres on the long edges of all four panels.

4 **Cutting the panels**
One panel at a time, saw the curve. Cut along the centre of the drawn line.

5 **Rebating the nose block**
Make a rebate around the edge of the nose block, 15 mm from the bottom.

7 **Gluing up**
Smear glue on all mating faces, fit the components together and clamp up.

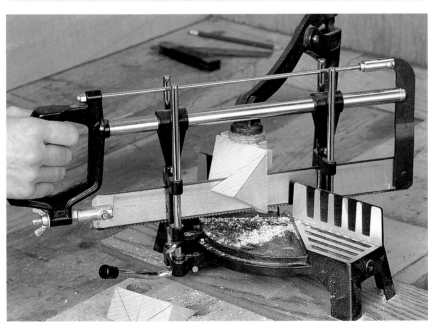

6 **Shaping the nose block**
Place the nose block in the mitre saw and on each side of the block make a cut from the bottom to the centre line – so that the nose is shaped into a pyramid, which has a rebate around its base to allow it to fit into the box.

TROUBLESHOOTING

- Before routing the panel mitres, practise on wood of the same thickness, to make sure that the mitres make a crisp 90° corner.

- Drill the core block in stages, running the bit in and right out, in order to avoid overheating the bit and burning the wood.

10: SWEDISH STORAGE TABLE

This beautiful storage table harks back to the storage boxes, dough boxes and food carriers that were traditionally made in Sweden in the last century. While it is basically no more than a box with a lid, the table is both functional and stylish. It performs two tasks, so if you are short of storage space and in need of a side table, this will fit the bill.

TOOLS AND MATERIALS

- workbench, fitted with a vice and holdfast
- square, tape measure, ruler, pencil
- backsaw
- screwdrivers: cross-point and flat
- bevel gauge
- router, 4 mm groove cutter, 45° mitre cutter
- jigsaw
- electric drill, 8 mm counter-bore bit, 8 mm plug cutter
- plane: smoothing and block planes
- sanding block and graded sandpaper
- screws: 24 x 20 mm cross-headed screws
- masking tape
- PVA glue
- Danish oil and beeswax polish
- birch plywood and maple (see cutting list)

CUTTING LIST

part	quantity	L x W x T
lid (A)	1	350 x 350 x 12.5
sides (B)	4	460 x 280 x 12.5
base (C)	1	207 x 207 x 4

All of the above are in birch plywood

legs (D) includes excess	4	590 x 30 x 30

All of the above are in maple

(finished sizes, given in millimetres)

This delightful little table-box is a winner on many counts. The design is modern and refreshingly simple, the tapered structure gives it an elegant appearance and, of course, you get two items of furniture – a storage box and a side table – for the price of one. What is more, it is easy to make. There is an optional hole in the lid for lifting it and if you also drill a hole in the base, you can neatly pass a lamp power cable through both.

WORKING DRAWINGS AND DETAIL OF THE SWEDISH STORAGE TABLE
measurements are given in millimetres

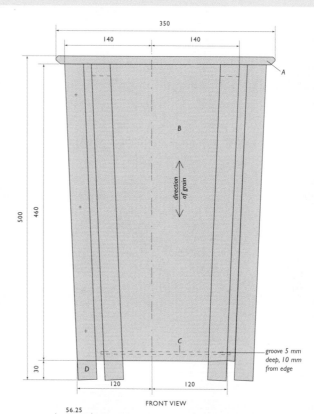

FRONT VIEW

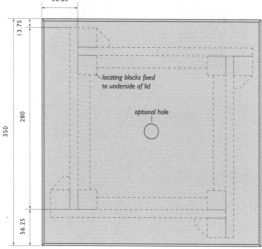

PLAN VIEW

DETAIL SHOWING THE INSIDE OF THE BOX

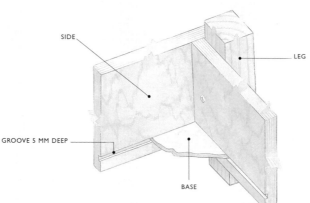

Design notes

The project is made up from ten parts – four plywood side boards, a plywood lid and base board, and four maple square sections that form the legs. The base is grooved into the side boards, and these are screwed to the maple sections. The lid board has four little offcuts screwed and glued to the underside to make location blocks, and it simply sits on top of the sides.

All the surfaces are sanded, sealed with Danish oil, rubbed down to remove the nibs of grain, and then waxed. Although the structure is relatively easy to make, the finish must be good – with well-placed screwholes, clean edges, and a crisp profile to the edge of the lid – if you want the end results to look professional.

Preparing the wood

Check the wood. Avoid having stains, splits or knots in crucial positions. Use the jigsaw and plane to cut and square the wood to size. Pencil-label the best faces of the plywood.

Making the sides

Draw out the side boards (460 mm long, 280 mm wide at the top, tapering to 240 mm wide at the base). Cut them out with the jigsaw. Work the sawn edges with the smoothing plane, to get rid of the rough finish (step 1).

Sand the sawn edges to a smooth finish with the sanding block and the graded sandpaper. Try to keep the sawn edges crisp and clean, with no rounding over of the corners. Finish with fine-grade sandpaper (step 2).

Fit the 4 mm groove cutter in the router. Set the fence to 10 mm and run each side board through to cut a groove on the inside face, 4 mm wide and 5 mm deep, 10 mm up from the bottom edge (step 3).

Putting together

Strap the four side boards together with masking tape, and mark in the position of the three screwholes along each edge. Drill the screwholes with the 8 mm counter-bore bit. Work at a steady pace, with the workpiece firmly clamped in position, in order to achieve accurately placed and cleanly cut holes (step 4).

Screw one edge of each panel to a leg, then fit the base board in the grooves and screw the other edges of the side boards to the legs so that the base is nicely contained. Cut the plugs with the 8 mm plug cutter and glue them into the counter-bored holes to cover up the screwheads (step 5).

Finishing

Use the bevel gauge to mark the top of the legs, making them level with the top of the side panels. Use the backsaw to saw off the top of the legs and plane to a smooth, level finish with the block plane. Bevel the top and bottom edges of the tabletop with the router and 45° mitre cutter, and sand to a smooth finish (step 6).

Glue and screw the offcuts from the legs to the underside of the tabletop to make location blocks. Finally, seal all the surfaces with a thin coat of Danish oil and let it dry. Rub down the nibs of grain with fine-grade sandpaper, and polish to a sheen finish with beeswax.

DESIGN VARIATIONS

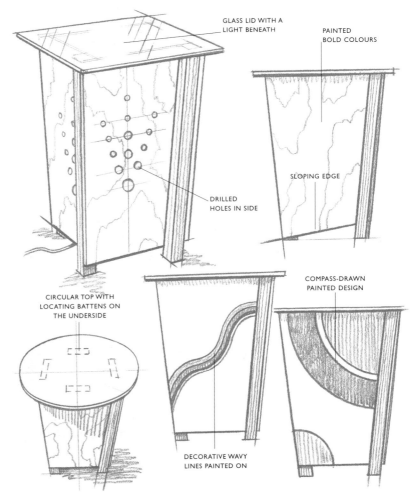

GLASS LID WITH A LIGHT BENEATH

PAINTED BOLD COLOURS

DRILLED HOLES IN SIDE

SLOPING EDGE

CIRCULAR TOP WITH LOCATING BATTENS ON THE UNDERSIDE

COMPASS-DRAWN PAINTED DESIGN

DECORATIVE WAVY LINES PAINTED ON

MAKING THE SWEDISH STORAGE TABLE

1 Shaping the side boards
Draw the side boards on the plywood. Check the measurements, and then cut out with the jigsaw. Use the smoothing plane to tidy up the sawn edges.

2 Sanding down
Use the sanding block and the graded sandpaper to rub the sawn edges to a smooth finish. Try not to blur the sharp edges.

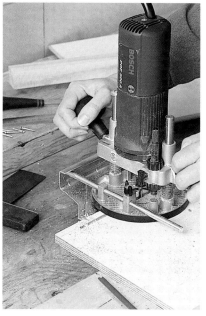

3 Grooving the base board
Fit the 4 mm groove cutter in the router, set the fence to 10 mm and cut a groove 4 mm wide, 5 mm deep and 10 mm up from the bottom edge.

4 Drilling screwholes
Strap the four sides together, and check that the screw positions are correctly marked. Run them through with the 8 mm counter-bore bit.

5 Putting together
Screw each side panel to a leg. Set the base board in place in the grooves and screw the other side of the panels to the legs. Glue plugs over the screwheads.

6 Mark off the top of the legs
Saw off the waste and plane the sawn face with the block plane.

TROUBLESHOOTING

- When you are marking out the screw positions, make sure that they are offset, so that the screws will not meet in the middle of the legs.

- Do not use excessive force to drive in the screws otherwise the heads may break off. If you are having difficulty, take out the screw and drill a larger pilot hole.

11: ARTS AND CRAFTS BLANKET BOX

This beautiful Arts and Crafts blanket box has not been designed to be made quickly and cheaply. It is made from top-quality oak, the handles have been painstakingly laminated and the dovetail joints have been hand-cut. If you have a desire to build an heirloom piece, and can dedicate lots of time to the project, this blanket box is both challenging and rewarding.

TOOLS AND MATERIALS

- workbench, fitted with a vice and holdfast
- square, steel tape measure, ruler, compass, pencil
- backsaw
- screwdrivers: cross-point and flat
- bevel gauge
- marking knife
- router, router table, 6 mm groove cutter
- jigsaw, dovetail saw, coping saw
- spokeshave
- planes: smoothing and block planes
- electric drill, 3 mm twist bit, 8 mm counter-bore bit, 8 mm plug cutter
- penknife
- chisel: 25 mm bevel-edged chisel and mallet
- clamps: 4 sash clamps
- power sander and graded sandpaper
- screws: 12 x 32 mm cross-headed screws for fixing handles, 4 x 19 mm round-headed countersunk screws for fixing straps
- hinges: 2 decorative steel strap hinges to suit, with screws to fit
- leather straps: 2 x 465 mm long and 400 mm wide
- PVA glue
- Danish oil and beeswax polish
- American white oak, oak veneer, birch plywood and pine (see cutting list)

WORKING DRAWINGS AND DETAIL OF THE ARTS AND CRAFTS BLANKET BOX *measurements are given in millimetres*

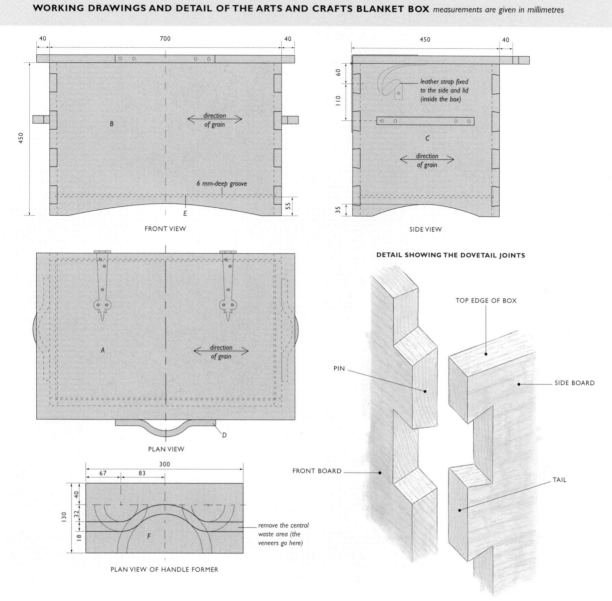

FRONT VIEW

SIDE VIEW

direction of grain

6 mm-deep groove

leather strap fixed to the side and lid (inside the box)

direction of grain

PLAN VIEW

direction of grain

DETAIL SHOWING THE DOVETAIL JOINTS

TOP EDGE OF BOX

PIN

SIDE BOARD

FRONT BOARD

TAIL

PLAN VIEW OF HANDLE FORMER

remove the central waste area (the veneers go here)

CUTTING LIST

part	quantity	L x W x T
lid (A)	1	780 x 490 x 23
front/back (B)	2	700 x 450 x 23
sides (C)	2	450 x 450 x 23
All of the above are in American white oak		
handles (D)	3	380 x 28 x 18
All of the above are in oak constructional veneer about 1.4 mm thick		
birch plywood base (E)	1	666 x 416 x 6
pine handle former (F)	1	300 x 130 x 28

(finished sizes, given in millimetres)

This blanket box was inspired by the Arts and Crafts movement of the early years of the twentieth century, when men such as Gustav Stickley in America and Ernest Gimson in England were making furniture that looked back to medieval traditions. Characteristically, the furniture was made from oak, with all the details worked by hand, and the structure and decoration considered as one and the same thing. Though the forms were simple, the designs paid great attention to detail and finish.

Design notes

There are nine component parts: front, back and side boards, the base board and lid, and three laminated handles. The base board is let into grooves in the front, back and side boards, which themselves are jointed with traditional dovetails. The handles are made from strips of laminated oak. The technique is easy: the strips are glued into a stack and clamped between two handle former blocks. When the glue has dried, the whole stack of strips holds the shape of the bridge. Take your time with this project, and don't be tempted to miss out the laminating. The dovetails and handles are the heart of the project.

Preparing the wood

Inspect the oak boards to make sure that they are free from splits. Use the jigsaw and smoothing plane to prepare the wood. Pencil-label the face side and edges, and mark them so that you know how they fit together. Stack the strips of veneer to make sure that you have enough to make three handles, each 18 mm thick (you will probably need thirteen layers for each handle).

Making the dovetail joints

Mark the shape of the pins on the ends of both sides of the front and back boards with the marking knife and bevel gauge (step 1).

Use the dovetail saw to cut down (on the waste side of) the scribed lines. Stop fractionally short of the gauged line (step 2).

Remove the waste with the coping saw. Clean up the pins with the chisel and penknife (step 3).

Set the pins on the ends of the side boards and score round them with the marking knife, forming the dovetails. Use the dovetail saw to clear the waste (step 4).

Continue to clear waste with the coping saw. Pare mating joints to a tight fit with the chisel (step 5).

Grooving front, back and sides

Fix the router to the router table and fit the 6 mm groove cutter. Adjust the fence to 55 mm. Pass all four boards through the router and cut a groove 6 mm wide, 6 mm deep, 55 mm up from the bottom edge.

Draw the shape of the arched foot on all four boards by springing the

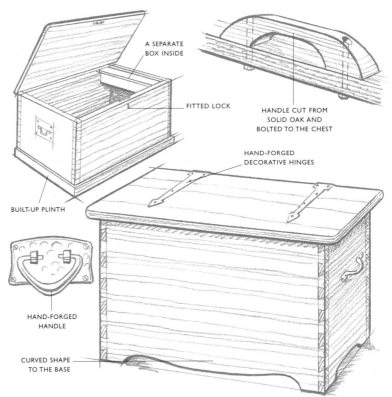

DESIGN VARIATIONS

A SEPARATE BOX INSIDE

FITTED LOCK

HANDLE CUT FROM SOLID OAK AND BOLTED TO THE CHEST

HAND-FORGED DECORATIVE HINGES

BUILT-UP PLINTH

HAND-FORGED HANDLE

CURVED SHAPE TO THE BASE

steel tape measure to make a bow. Cut the curve with the jigsaw. Use the spokeshave to bring the sawn edge to a good finish (step 6).

Putting together

Have a trial dry run, then glue all mating faces. Knock one side board on to the front and back boards, so that the side board locks them in place. Slide the base board down the grooves. Fit the other side board. If you need to use the mallet, don't strike the oak directly and bruise the wood – use buffers of scrap wood. Level the joints with the chisel, smoothing and block planes (step 7).

Laminating the handles

Using the jigsaw, fret out the shape of the bridge handle on the piece of pine, so you have two pieces of wood that make the handle former. Stack oak

strips together to make a total thickness of 18 mm. Glue the strips to make a wood-and-glue sandwich, set them in the former and clamp up with sash clamps. Repeat the procedure to make three identical handles. Plane the handles with the smoothing and block planes, and sand to a good finish with sandpaper. The handles should now be 23 mm wide (step 8).

Drill holes for the screws with the 8 mm counter-bore bit. Screw the handles in place on the chest. Cut plugs with the 8 mm plug cutter and glue them over the screwheads. Drill pilot holes for the hinges with the 3 mm twist bit, then fit the lid to the box with the hinges. Sand the box with the power sander, coat with Danish oil and burnish with beeswax. Finally, screw the leather support straps in place on the inside of the lid with the 19 mm screws.

MAKING THE ARTS AND CRAFTS BLANKET BOX

1 Marking out the dovetail pins
Mark out the shape of the pins on both sides of the ends of the front and back boards. Shade in the waste so that you know what needs cutting away.

2 Sawing the pins
Run the cut so that it stops fractionally short of the gauged line.

3 Sawing out the waste
With the coping saw, continue the cut until the piece of waste falls clear.

4 Sawing the dovetails
Transfer the shape of the pins on to the side boards – so that the shape of the dovetails is clearly set out. Use the dovetail saw to cut out.

5 Cutting out the waste
Clear the waste with the coping saw and pare edges with the chisel.

6 Cutting the arched sides
Cut out the waste with the jigsaw. Use the spokeshave to smooth the finish.

7 Putting together
Glue all mating faces. Knock a side board on to the front and back boards. Slide the base board down the grooves, and fit the other side board.

8 Laminating the handles
Glue the strips into a sandwich, put in the handle former and clamp up.

TROUBLESHOOTING

• When you are fitting the joints, do not make them so tight that they split the wood. They just need to be a tight push-fit.

• When you are clamping up the strips for the handles, do it slowly to allow the strips to bend gradually and move into position.

12: WOVEN WOOD LAUNDRY BOX

If you enjoy experimenting with wood, you will get a lot of pleasure from this project. The design owes something to the Swedish and American Shaker traditions of making carriers, with perhaps a sideways look to the English garden trug. The box is functional and decorative – perfect for a modern home.

TOOLS AND MATERIALS

- workbench, fitted with a vice and holdfast
- square, tape measure, ruler, pencil
- backsaw
- screwdrivers: cross-point and flat
- router, 6 mm template profile cutter, 4 mm groove cutter, curve-following wheel attachment
- jigsaw
- bench drill press and forstner bits, 12.5 mm, 30 mm
- electric drill, small pilot-countersink bit
- clamps: 2 G-clamps
- graded sandpaper
- screws: 6 x 25 mm countersunk screws
- 450 mm length of 12.5 mm dowel (includes wastage)
- PVA glue
- Danish oil and beeswax polish
- birch plywood and ash (see cutting list)

CUTTING LIST

part	quantity	L x W x T
lid (A)	1	358 x 348 x 9.5
top and base plates (B)	2	358 x 348 x 19

All of the above are in birch plywood and the dimensions allow for wastage

ash posts (C)	3	508 x 29 x 29
ash long slats (D)	27	524 x 30 x 3
ash short slats (E)	9	304 x 30 x 3

(finished sizes, given in millimetres)

While this box has been designed as a bedroom laundry box – hence the woven structure that allows airflow around the fabrics inside – the design is so decorative that the box could equally be used in the main living area as a little side table. The woven wood is also reminiscent of traditional pieces of furniture such as wicker and cane chairs, so perhaps it could find a place as a storage table in the garden room or conservatory.

Design notes

Each box side is made up from twelve strips of ash, three horizontal and nine vertical, which are woven together to make a panel. The top and bottom edges of the vertical strips are contained in the groove in the triangular top and base plates, and the ends of the horizontal strips are held in dash grooves in the corner uprights. This project may look quite difficult, but it is quite straightforward if you select the ash with care, and avoid wood that looks in any way split, knotty or twisted.

Preparing the wood

Inspect the wood thoroughly, especially the ash slats that form the woven sides. Check each slat to make sure that it is smooth along its length, with no knots or splits along the edges. Flex each slat to make sure that it is supple and springy. Saw and plane the wood to size (see pages 10–12).

Making the base, top, lid and corner posts

Although the base, top and lid pieces are identical in overall shape, the base and the top are 19 mm thick, while the lid is only 9.5 mm thick. Cut out the triangular lid with the jigsaw, and sand the edges to a smooth finish with

WORKING DRAWINGS AND DETAIL OF THE WOVEN WOOD LAUNDRY BOX
measurements are given in millimetres

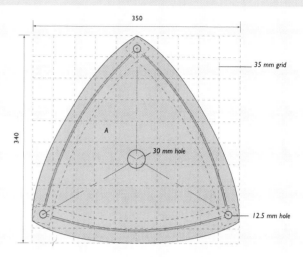

PLAN VIEW

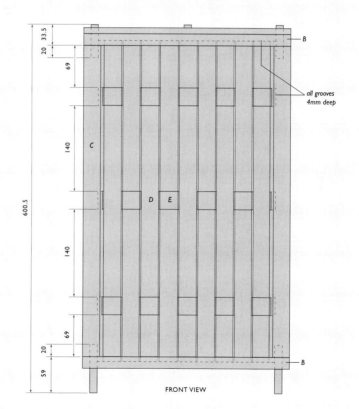

FRONT VIEW

DETAIL SHOWING THE INSIDE OF A CORNER AT THE TOP OF THE BOX

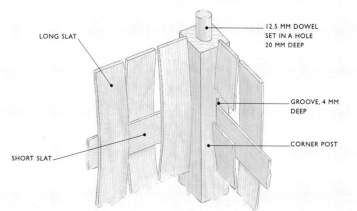

sandpaper. Drill holes at the lid corners and centre with the bench drill press. Use the 12.5 mm forstner bit for the corners and the 30 mm bit for the centre (step 1).

Cut out the other two triangles for the base and top, making them about 4 mm oversize. Clamp the finished lid on top of these and use the router with the wheel attachment and the 6 mm template profile cutter to trim the other two triangles to shape and size (step 2).

Use the router and the 4 mm groove cutter to groove the base and top triangles. Set the wheel attachment and fence to 22 mm. Working on the top of the base triangle, and the underside of the top triangle, cut grooves 8 mm deep, 22 mm from the bottom edge (step 3).

With the bench drill press and 30 mm forstner bit, drill a pilot hole by each corner of the waste area of the top triangle, and cut to the drawn line with the jigsaw. Rub down the sawn edge with sandpaper (step 4).

Drill holes at each end of the three corner posts. Two at a time, clamp the posts together and use the router with the 4 mm groove cutter (set the router fence so that it is centred on one post) to cut three dash-grooves on mating faces – six grooves on each post (step 5).

Making the woven sides

Take eight uprights and three horizontal slats and weave them together so that the uprights are side by side (with a small gap in between each to accommodate the movement in the wood – without the gap the panel may bow), and the horizontal slats are spaced to align with the dash-grooves in the posts. Re-run this procedure for all three woven panels (step 6).

Putting together and finishing

Glue and plug the ends of the posts with the dowels (79 mm long at the foot end and 53.5 mm at the top). Slide the foot end dowels into the holes in the base board, and the top dowels into the top board. Make sure that the grooved side of the base is uppermost. Set the woven panels in place, with the bottom ends of the slats pushed in the groove on the base, and ease the ends of the horizontal slats into the dash-grooves in the upright posts (step 7).

Slide the top triangle in place, with the grooves on the underside, and ease the top ends of the slats into the grooves. Fix the top and base triangles to the posts using the electric drill and pilot-countersink bit to make screw-holes. Run the holes through the corners of the top and base triangles and into the dowels mounted in the posts. Screw the top and the base to the posts with the six countersunk screws. Finally, seal the laundry box with a coat of Danish oil, and polish with beeswax.

DESIGN VARIATIONS

CORNER BOX WITH JUST THE FRONT SLATTED AND THE OTHER TWO SIDES MADE OF PLYWOOD

SQUARE BOX WITH WOVEN SLATS ON ALL FOUR SIDES

TRIANGULAR BOX (THE CORNER POSTS WOULD BE MORE OF A CHALLENGE TO MAKE)

OCTAGONAL BOX WITH THREE VERTICAL SLATS PER SIDE

HEXAGONAL BOX

SQUARE POST

SQUARE POST

MAKING THE WOVEN WOOD LAUNDRY BOX

1 Drilling holes in the lid
Fret out the triangular lid board with the jigsaw, and use the bench drill press to bore out the holes – 12.5 mm at the corners and 30 mm at the centre.

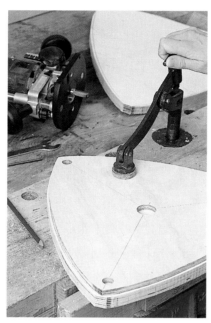

2 Routing the duplicate triangles
Clamp the lid on top of the base and top boards. Use the router, wheel attachment and template profile cutter to trim the other boards to size.

3 Grooving the triangles
Cut grooves on the top of the base, and the underside of the top board.

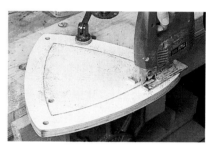

4 Cutting out the top
Drill a hole by each corner of the waste area. Saw between the holes.

5 Dash-grooving the posts
Clamp a pair of posts together, centre the groove cutter on one post, and then plunge three cuts on mating faces. Repeat for all three posts.

6 Weaving the sides
Divide the long slats into groups of eight and set them side by side. Weave three horizontals through each group and align with the dash-grooved posts.

7 Putting together
Fit the woven panels in the grooves in the base and posts.

TROUBLESHOOTING

- Use flexible wood for the slats, which is completely free of knots and edge splits.

- Putting the box together is much easier if you have a helper.

- It's always a good idea, if you are at all unsure of a technique, to have a try-out on some scrap wood.

13: STASH-IT-ALL BOXES

O ur office was submerged by an avalanche of paperclips, pens, pencils, printing ink and all sorts of other essential bits and pieces. Wondering how we could sort out the mess, hide it away but keep it accessible, we came up with the idea of building a set of "tidy" boxes.

TOOLS AND MATERIALS

- workbench, fitted with a vice and holdfast
- square, tape measure, ruler, pencil
- backsaw
- router, router table and 4 mm, 6 mm and 13 mm groove cutters
- bench drill press and 20 mm forstner drill bit
- block plane
- clamps: 4 G-clamps or similar
- power sander and graded sandpaper
- PVA glue
- Danish oil and beeswax polish
- cherry and birch plywood (see cutting list)

CUTTING LIST

part	quantity	L x W x T
side (A)	4	236 x 180 x 10
top/bottom (B)	2	230 x 180 x 10
top/bottom (C)	2	338 x 180 x 10
division (D)	1	324 x 162 x 6
division (E)	2	216 x 162 x 6
division (F)	3	116 x 162 x 6
division (G)	1	108 x 162 x 6
drawer front/back (H)	4	208 x 108 x 10
drawer front/back (I)	6	100 x 108 x 10
drawer side (J)	10	152 x 108 x 10
drawer front/back (K)	4	208 x 50 x 10
drawer front/back (L)	4	100 x 50 x 10
drawer side (M)	8	152 x 50 x 10

All of the above are in cherry

back (N)	1	218 x 234 x 4
back (O)	1	326 x 234 x 4
drawer bottom (P)	4	150 x 196 x 4
drawer bottom (Q)	5	150 x 88 x 4

All of the above are in birch plywood

(finished sizes, given in millimetres)

The boxes are ideal for holding bits and pieces. The drawers come in four different sizes, the finger holes are nicely considered, the two units make for a flexible arrangement and the boxes look good sitting at the back of a desk. The units can be placed one on top of another, or screwed side by side to the wall, or you can make numerous sets and stack them together on a desk or shelf.

WORKING DRAWINGS AND DETAIL OF THE STASH-IT-ALL BOXES *measurements are given in millimetres*

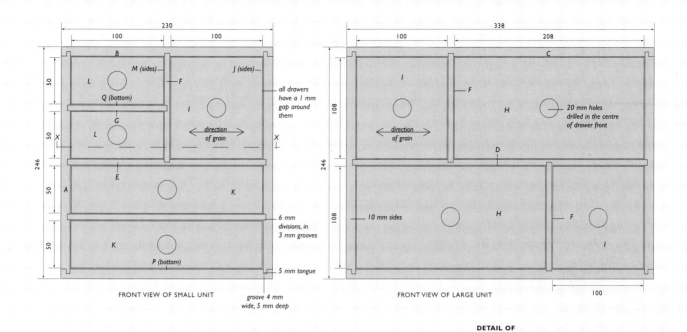

FRONT VIEW OF SMALL UNIT

FRONT VIEW OF LARGE UNIT

all drawers have a 1 mm gap around them

direction of grain

6 mm divisions, in 3 mm grooves

5 mm tongue

groove 4 mm wide, 5 mm deep

20 mm holes drilled in the centre of drawer front

10 mm sides

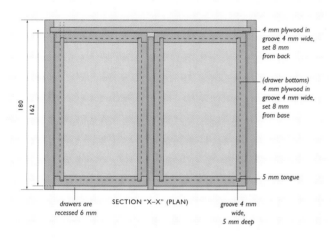

SECTION "X–X" (PLAN)

drawers are recessed 6 mm

4 mm plywood in groove 4 mm wide, set 8 mm from back

(drawer bottoms) 4 mm plywood in groove 4 mm wide, set 8 mm from base

5 mm tongue

groove 4 mm wide, 5 mm deep

DETAIL OF DRAWER CONSTRUCTION

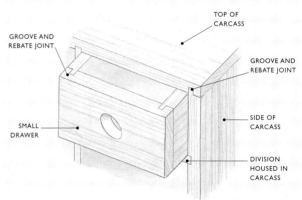

GROOVE AND REBATE JOINT

SMALL DRAWER

TOP OF CARCASS

GROOVE AND REBATE JOINT

SIDE OF CARCASS

DIVISION HOUSED IN CARCASS

Design notes

The design is based on a cube module, with the various drawers being either one-cube, or two-cube rectilinear. The component parts are variously rebated and grooved with the router cutters. The drawers are designed so that they are set back in the carcass, the idea being that the shadow line not only strengthens the appearance, but draws the eye away from a possible loose fit. Note how the drawers are interchangeable.

Preparing the wood

Saw and plane the wood to size (see pages 10–12). Label the components with a pencil. Use the square, ruler and pencil to draw in the position of all the grooves, rebates and housings. Separate all the component parts into two groups: one group for the drawers for the small unit and the large unit, and another group for the carcasses of both units. Try and keep these groups separate throughout the making procedure.

Routing the joints

Attach the router to its table and fit the 4 mm groove cutter. Set the fence for cutting the corner joint grooves on the top and bottom carcass boards. When you are sure that all is correct, switch on the router, and make three passes to cut each groove, gradually getting deeper, until the groove is 5 mm deep (step 1).

Cut 4 mm grooves for the back board in the top, bottom and side carcass boards (step 2).

To cut the carcass rebates at the end of the side boards, fit the 13 mm groove cutter. Set the fence to 6 mm, so that the rebate extends 5 mm from the end of the board. Run the boards through to cut a rebate 5 mm wide and 6 mm deep (step 3).

Use the 6 mm cutter to make the 3 mm-deep housing grooves in the carcasses (for the divisions).

The drawers are made in the same way as the carcasses.

Drilling finger holes

Draw crossed diagonals on all the drawer fronts to establish the centres of the finger holes. Fit the 20 mm forstner bit in the bench drill press, support the workpiece on a piece of scrap wood, and run the holes through. Work at a steady pace to make sure that the drill bit enters and exits cleanly (step 4).

Putting together

Take the boards that go to make up the carcass and have a trial fitting before gluing. Then dribble glue in the housing and rebate grooves, set the back board and the dividing boards in place (dry), locate the rebate tongues in the grooves and clamp up (step 5).

Re-run the same procedure for the drawers, making sure that the drawer base is fitted dry (step 6).

Finishing

When the glue is dry, remove the clamps and bring all the edges and faces to a good finish. Work on the drawers first, using the block plane to plane the end grain flush so the drawer fits easily into the carcass. Use the power sander on the drawer faces, and sandpaper on the edges. When you are sanding, be careful not to round over the edges (step 7).

Finish the carcass by planing the end grain flush with the boards, working at an angle. Sand the carcass faces with the power sander and rub the edges by hand with sandpaper. Pay particular attention to the top and sides of the carcasses. Make sure the fronts of the drawers are sanded to perfection (step 8).

Wipe away the dust and debris and move to a clean area. Brush the boxes with Danish oil and leave to dry.

Fit the drawers in place and see how they move in and out. If they now stick, identify the problem and resolve it either by sanding the inside of the carcass, or by planing and scraping a little wood off the drawers. Repair the finish afterwards.

Finally, sand all the surfaces with the finest sandpaper to remove the nibs of grain, and use beeswax to polish to a sheen finish.

DESIGN VARIATIONS

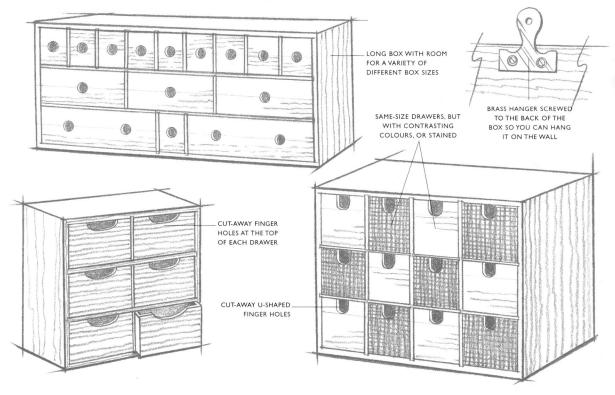

LONG BOX WITH ROOM FOR A VARIETY OF DIFFERENT BOX SIZES

BRASS HANGER SCREWED TO THE BACK OF THE BOX SO YOU CAN HANG IT ON THE WALL

SAME-SIZE DRAWERS, BUT WITH CONTRASTING COLOURS, OR STAINED

CUT-AWAY FINGER HOLES AT THE TOP OF EACH DRAWER

CUT-AWAY U-SHAPED FINGER HOLES

MAKING THE STASH-IT-ALL BOXES

1 Routing the corner grooves
Take a carcass board, centre the cutter on a corner groove and make the cut.

2 Routing grooves for the back
Run the boards through lengthwise making a groove 8 mm in from the edge.

3 Routing the carcass rebates
Use the 13 mm groove cutter to cut a rebate 6 mm deep and 5 mm wide.

4 Drilling the finger holes
Drill through the crossed diagonals, supporting the workpiece with scrap.

5 Gluing up the carcass
Smear glue on the tongues and in the housing grooves, set the back board (dry) in place in the groove and clamp the whole thing together.

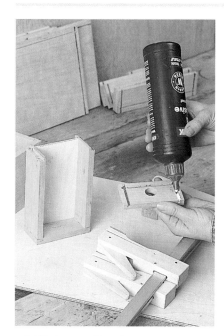

6 Gluing up the drawers
Smear glue on the tongues, set the base board in the groove dry, bring the four boards together, check for squareness and gently clamp up.

7 Planing the drawers
Use the block plane to plane the end grain flush so that the drawer fits into the carcass easily. Be careful not to split off the side grain. Finish by sanding.

8 Planing the carcass
Plane the end grain flush with the boards and sand to a good finish.

TROUBLESHOOTING

- If you are a beginner, it might be an idea to make the carcass first and then make the drawers to fit.
- Avoid wiping away oozes of glue with a cloth. It is much better to leave it to dry, and then remove it with a chisel or plane.

14: STACKING STORAGE BOXES

I f, like us, your house is awash with books, papers, tools, toys and all manner of other collectibles, these boxes are going to come in very useful. Simply fill up each box to bursting, stack them one upon another, and put them in a spare corner. Make three, six, or as many boxes as you need!

TOOLS AND MATERIALS

- workbench, fitted with a vice and holdfast
- square, tape measure, ruler, compass, pencil
- backsaw
- screwdrivers: cross-point and flat
- router, router table, 4 mm groove cutter, 16 mm template profile cutter
- jigsaw
- bench drill press, 4 mm twist bit, and 5 mm, 10 mm and 15 mm forstner drill bits
- spokeshave
- power sander and graded sandpaper
- masking tape
- screws: 72 x 20 mm self-tapping, slotted pan-headed screws
- acrylic paint in colour to suit, 25 mm paintbrush
- PVA glue
- Danish oil and beeswax polish
- birch plywood and beech (see cutting list)

CUTTING LIST

part	quantity	L x W x T
birch plywood sides (A)	12	340 x 340 x 6
birch plywood bases (B)	3	346 x 346 x 4
beech posts (C)	12	340 x 20 x 20

(finished sizes, given in millimetres)

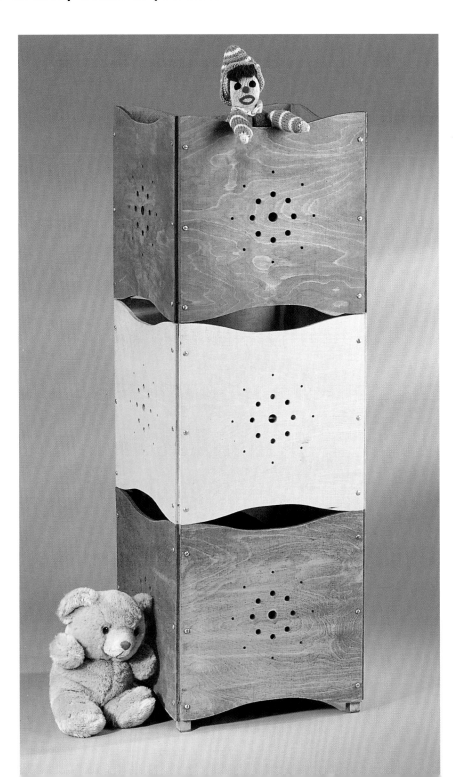

Our design brief for the boxes was that they should be identical, inexpensive and very easy to make. The idea is that additional boxes can be made at short notice. So if you have children with a jungle of toys, teenagers with lots of sports kit or an office-study that is outgrowing its space, you simply make a repeat order of boxes to suit your needs. If you like the overall notion of the project but want to cut costs – or only need rough boxes for a shed or garage – you could opt for using a lower grade of plywood instead of birch plywood.

Design notes

Each box is made from nine component parts, with the side boards being grooved to take the base board. The side boards are screwed to the square corner sections in such a way that the revealed plywood edges of the side boards become a design feature.

The wavy concave profile at the top and bottom edges of each side board is both decorative and functional, in that it creates a handle-like hole that allows you to stack the boxes without any danger of nipping your fingers. The holes in the box sides also have a dual purpose – they form a pattern that adds interest, but also function as airholes, so the contents don't become damp or mouldy.

Preparing the wood

Check that there are no stains or delamination in the wood, then use the jigsaw to cut the wood to length and width. Pencil-label each side, best face and top edge. If you notice that a piece of plywood has patched knot holes or particularly wild grain that does not match the rest of the pieces, make sure that the offending surface is positioned to face inward.

WORKING DRAWINGS AND DETAIL OF THE STACKING STORAGE BOXES
measurements are given in millimetres

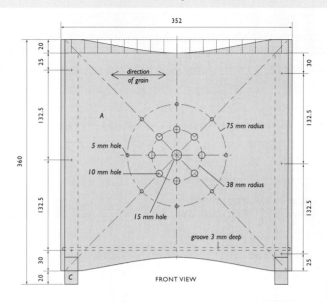

FRONT VIEW

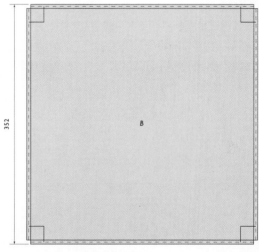

PLAN VIEW

EXPLODED DETAIL SHOWING THE BOTTOM CORNER FROM INSIDE THE BOX

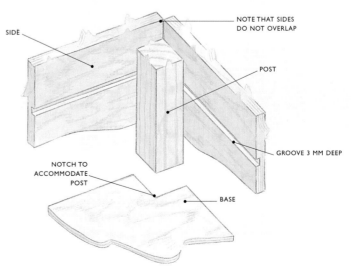

Drilling and grooving the sides

Strap a batch of side boards together with masking tape, draw diagonals to establish the centre point, then draw out the 45° radial grid. Draw two circles, one with a radius of 38 mm and the other 75 mm. The intersections of the circles and the 45° guidelines mark the position of the drill holes (step 1).

Drill out the holes with the bench drill press. Use the 15 mm forstner bit for the centre, the 10 mm bit for the inner circle and the 5 mm bit on the outer circle. Run the screwholes through with the 4 mm twist bit. Fit the router to its table, insert the 4 mm groove cutter, and set the fence to 30 mm. Undo the stack of boards and run them through one at a time to cut a groove 4 mm wide, 3 mm deep and 30 mm up from the edge (step 2).

Routing the curved edges

Take one side board and use the jigsaw, spokeshave and sandpaper to cut the curved profile to a crisp, smooth finish (step 3).

Use the jigsaw to cut the bulk of the waste from the other boards, so that the sawn edge is within about 5 mm of the drawn line. Clamp the finished side board under one of the part-finished boards, fit the router with the 16 mm template profile cutter and follow the underside board (the template board) to cut the other edge to a finish. Re-run this procedure with all the boards (step 4).

Putting together and finishing

Take a base board and use the jigsaw to cut notches from each corner. Make them 23 mm square. Do this with all the base boards (step 5).

Take the side boards and screw them one at a time to a beech post (one board to one post), so that the edge of the board is flush with the edge of the post. Arrange the side boards, with the base contained in the groove, and screw them together to make the box. If the sides are reluctant to go together, plane the edges of the base and cut the corner notches slightly bigger (or you might have to make the grooves wider) (step 6).

Use the power sander to bring all the surfaces to a smooth finish, then clean up the dust and debris. Paint the wood with the colour of your choice (or leave it unpainted if you prefer a natural wood finish). Leave to dry, then rub down with fine-grade sandpaper to remove the nibs of grain. Seal with Danish oil and polish to a sheen finish with beeswax.

DESIGN VARIATIONS

WORKSHOP BOX REINFORCED BY METAL CORNER STRAPS, WITH NATURAL FINISH AND HANDLE HOLES CUT IN THE SIDES

MORE HOLES OF DIFFERENT SIZES TO FORM A CROSS ON THE SIDES OF THE BOX

A STENCILLED DESIGN IN THREE COLOURS

BOLD GEOMETRIC PAINTED DESIGN

A PIERCED DESIGN MADE WITH DRILLED HOLES AND A JIGSAW

THE BASE CUT AWAY SLIGHTLY

MAKING THE STACKING STORAGE BOXES

1 Marking the holes

Strap a batch of side boards together with masking tape, draw diagonals to establish the centre point, then mark out guidelines at 45° intervals. Use the compass at a radius of 38 mm, and then at 75 mm, to draw two circles. The intersections between the circles and the guidelines mark the position of the holes.

2 Drilling the holes in the sides

Use the bench drill press and the forstner bit to make holes: 15 mm at the centre, 10 mm on the inner circle, and 5 mm on the outer circle.

3 Shaping the curves

Take one side board and use the jigsaw to fret out the basic shape. Use the spokeshave and the sandpaper to bring the curved edges to a good finish.

4 Duplicating the curves

Use a finished board as a template and cut with the template profile cutter.

5 Notching the corners

Cut out a 23 mm square in each corner of the base board with the jigsaw.

6 Screwing together

Screw one post to one side of each side board. Screw the sides together.

TROUBLESHOOTING

• When you are screwing the side boards to the posts, make sure that the edges are flush, so that the finished boxes show a notch at the corners.

• When you are drilling the stack of boards, put them on a piece of waste wood, so that the exit holes are crisp.

15: STORAGE TRAY

magine that you are engrossed in some intricate pursuit such as sewing or jewellery-making, working on your lap. Suddenly visitors arrive and you need to store away all your bits and pieces quickly. This storage tray comes to the rescue, keeping all the components safely together and organized.

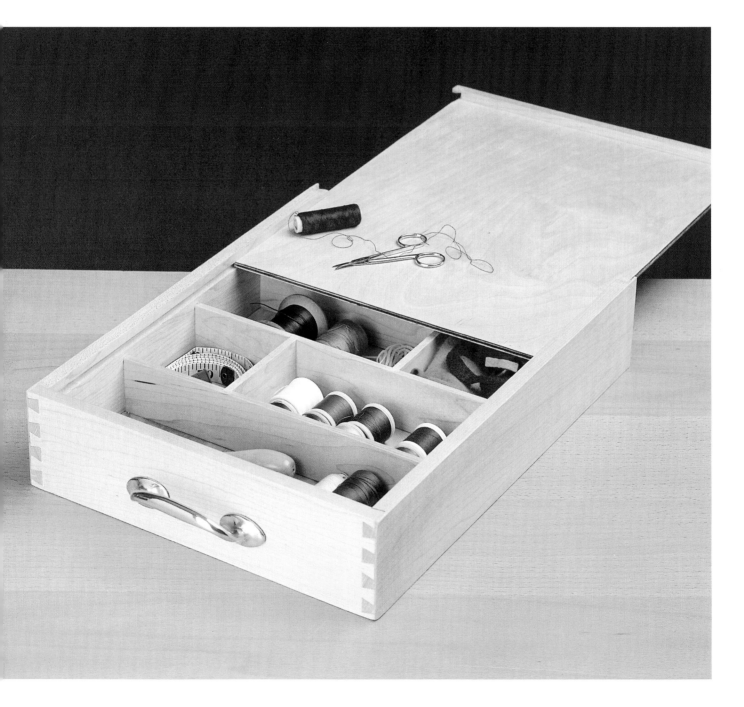

WORKING DRAWINGS AND DETAIL OF THE STORAGE TRAY
measurements are given in millimetres

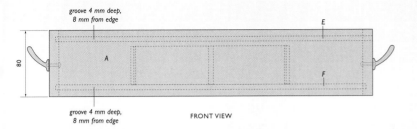

groove 4 mm deep,
8 mm from edge

80

A

E

F

groove 4 mm deep,
8 mm from edge

FRONT VIEW

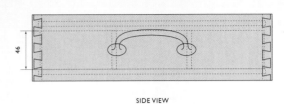

46

SIDE VIEW

**EXPLODED DETAIL OF THE TRAY
CORNER SHOWING THE DOVETAIL JOINTS
(VIEWED FROM THE INSIDE)**

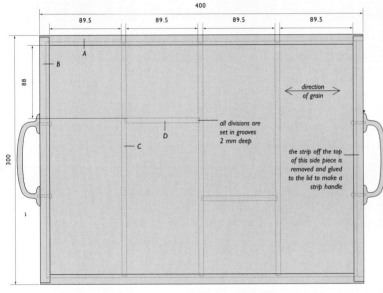

400

89.5   89.5   89.5   89.5

A

B

88

300

C

D

*direction
of grain*

*all divisions are
set in grooves
2 mm deep*

*the strip off the top
of this side piece is
removed and glued
to the lid to make a
strip handle*

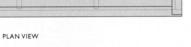

PLAN VIEW

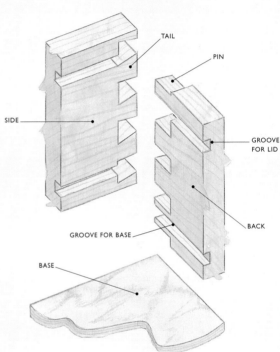

TAIL

PIN

SIDE

GROOVE
FOR LID

GROOVE FOR BASE

BACK

BASE

TOOLS AND MATERIALS

- workbench, fitted with a vice and holdfast
- square, tape measure, ruler, pencil
- backsaw
- screwdrivers: cross-point and flat
- router, router table, 6 mm groove cutter
- electric drill and dovetailing attachment with grid clamp
- block plane
- chisel: bevel-edged, 13 mm

- whittling knife
- clamps: 2 sash clamps
- graded sandpaper
- handles: 2 x 120 mm brass handles with screws to fit
- PVA glue
- Danish oil and beeswax polish
- maple and birch plywood (see cutting list)

CUTTING LIST

part	quantity	L x W x T
maple front/back (A)	2	400 x 80 x 12
maple sides (B)	2	296 x 80 x 12
maple long divisions (C)	3	280 x 46 x 6
maple short divisions (D)	2	93.5 x 46 x 6
birch plywood lid (E)	1	392 x 284 x 6
birch plywood base (F)	1	384 x 284 x 6

(finished sizes, given in millimetres)

The clever thing about this tray is the way that the top slides back to reveal all the pigeonhole compartments. It is perfect for any task or hobby that requires lots of small components. Embroiderers, for example, would find it ideal for all their needles, pins and hanks of embroidery thread.

Design notes

The tray is made from eleven component parts – the base board and lid board, the front, back and sides that comprise the main frame, and the five strips that divide the area inside. The corners of the frame are jointed with machine dovetails, while all other parts are housed in grooves. The traditional cast-brass tray handles are bolted from the inside.

The sizes of the various honeycomb holes have been chosen to accommodate the paraphernalia of sewing and embroidery. However, you might want to modify the sizes to suit your requirements.

Preparing the wood

Check that the wood is in good condition, with no loose knots, stains, splits or uncharacteristic grain. Measure and square the wood to length and width (see pages 10–12). Pencil-label all the face sides and edges of the components, and mark them so that you know how they relate to one another.

Dovetailing the frame

Take the front of the tray and clamp it to the bench with the grid clamp, so you are set up for cutting the pins into the end grain. Attach the dovetailing attachment to the electric drill and run the cutter straight into the grid to clear the waste from between the pins. Re-run this procedure for both ends of the front and back (step 1).

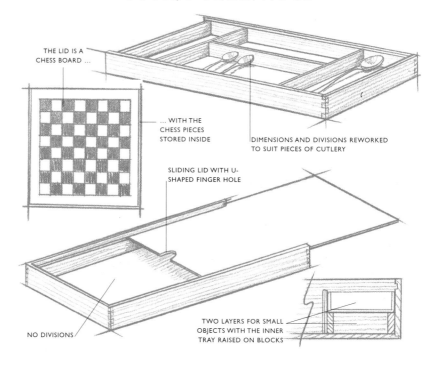

DESIGN VARIATIONS

THE LID IS A CHESS BOARD ...

... WITH THE CHESS PIECES STORED INSIDE

DIMENSIONS AND DIVISIONS REWORKED TO SUIT PIECES OF CUTLERY

SLIDING LID WITH U-SHAPED FINGER HOLE

NO DIVISIONS

TWO LAYERS FOR SMALL OBJECTS WITH THE INNER TRAY RAISED ON BLOCKS

To cut the dovetails, set one of the tray side boards on a piece of waste, position the front board on top of it, and locate the two guide knobs on the grid clamp either side of the pins that you have already cut. Tighten up the clamps and plunge down to cut the dovetails. Do this on both ends of all the side boards. Use a knife to trim the dovetails to a good fit (step 2).

Cutting grooves

Attach the router to its table and fit the 6 mm groove cutter. Set the fence for 8 mm and run grooves along the inside face and on both edges of the front, back and sides of the tray, making the grooves for the base and lid. Saw a strip off the top of one side board (see working drawing) to make a strip handle for the lid (step 3).

Mark in the position of all the housing grooves on the inside face of the front and back, and on the appropriate sides of the dividing strips.

Clamp the boards flat on the bench with a fence strip across the width to act as a guide for the router, and then rout them through. Re-run this procedure for all the cross grooves (step 4).

Putting together

Take the component parts, all jointed and grooved, and rub them down with fine-grade sandpaper to remove all rough edges. Glue all mating faces. Take the front board, slide the base board into the groove, fit the divisions together and locate them in the housing grooves (step 5).

Knock the other sides of the box together so that the divisions are contained, and clamp up. Glue the strip handle on top of the lid board, and fit the brass handles. Trim to a good finish with the block plane and the bevel-edged chisel. Brush a thin coat of Danish oil over the whole tray, rub down with fine-grade sandpaper, and burnish with beeswax (step 6).

MAKING THE STORAGE TRAY

Cutting lid and base grooves
Groove the tray front and back, first one side and then the other.

1 Cutting the pins
Position the tray front on the bench. Slide the grid clamp in place and tighten up. Run the cutter straight into the end grain to cut the pins.

2 Cutting the dovetails
Set one of the tray sides on the bench, complete with its matching front/back (pins already cut). Clamp the grid attachment and cut the dovetails.

4 Cutting the housing grooves
Centre the cutter on the marked-out grooves, and then rout the groove.

6 Assembling the frame
Knock the other three sides of the box together and clamp up.

TROUBLESHOOTING

• Though dovetailing attachments work on more or less the same principle, you will need to read the manufacturer's guide manual in order to fine-tune the techniques.

• Prior to gluing, it is sensible to have a dry-run fitting, to make sure that the parts all come together properly.

5 Assembling the base
Remove all the dust and debris from the grooves, and clean the working area. Slide the base board in the groove in the front board, and fit the dividing strips together, locating the ends in the appropriate grooves.

INDEX